Snapped! Comments From a C-c-conservative

Snippets, Volume 4

Phil Berto

Published by Stormy Summers Publishing, 2019.

While every precaution has been taken in the preparation of this book, the publisher assumes no responsibility for errors or omissions, or for damages resulting from the use of the information contained herein.

SNAPPED! COMMENTS FROM A C-C-CONSERVATIVE

First edition. December 30, 2019.

Copyright © 2019 Phil Berto.

Written by Phil Berto.

Also by Phil Berto

Snippets
Snippets: Comments from the Red
Snipped: America Post #Metoo
SNIPS: Comments from The Black and Blue
Snapped! Comments From a C-c-conservative

Watch for more at www.philberto.com.

DEDICATION

JUST DO IT: Someone at Nike should read Kaepernick the rest of the Frederick Douglass letter. Meanwhile, I'm buying Adidas.

UN-DEDICATION

THE PELOSI PEROGATIVE: We can't beat Trump in 2020. Impeachment didn't work, and we don't have the votes to abolish the Electoral College. Hey, Moe! Let's forbid voting in Kansas, Nebraska, Oklahoma and Utah. Yeah, that's it!

Q: Nancy. Buddy. Doesn't "Democrat" mean everyone votes?

A: As MEgan said: "Only those who agree with us".

OCEAN BREEZES AND HOT AIR:

Q: When will Martha's Vineyard get windmills?

A: When Aspen gets a Martin Luther King Boulevard. Do-dah.

FINAL THOUGHT

Plants and animals evolve at the pleasure of their Maker.

Man was custom made by God. <u>What was He thinking</u>?

SNAPPED! Comments from a c-c-conservative

FOREWORD

Much of what you are about to read has appeared online (a Snippet at a time) to, we believe, some effect.

Many Americans have stopped spouting euphemisms like "women's health issue" and "freedom of choice"; they now call late-term and partial-birth abortion what they are: infanticide.

Folks now question why able-bodied deadbeats who spend their food money on tattoos and body bling are "entitled" to food stamps, parasitically paid for with Other People's Money by faceless bureaucrats whose own grotesque existence is enabled by a system that sustains itself on the backs of working people.

Kammy and Beto have withdrawn their candidacies, as we predicted. Joe is self-destructing, and Pocahontas can't stop lying. The left is eating its own, as it always does, but <u>too late</u>: they have already exposed themselves for the frauds and ninnies they are.

Can we prove that we brought about their demise? Nope.

Do we think we had a hand in outing their self-serving agenda?

You bet we do.

Phil Berto

Christmas, 2019

Purgatory (Northflorida)

PS: The biggest fraud of all, who got herself elected by some dumbass voters without using her real name, lives on via our Gillibrand Glossary. Look it up.

This just in:

NO SHIT

A product now exists that prevents Fido from eating feces. Sprinkle it on, and even cat shit will seem disgusting to him.

Q: What's IN this stuff?

A: Tofu. (Read the label)

How nice! Now, when Bowser licks baby's face, the worst thing he has just eaten will be his own asshole. Sanctitys of Motherhood everywhere will be so pleased.

GALA
UNELECTED
BUREAUCRAT SECTION
################

H OW DOES IT FEEL? Bob Dylan, <u>A Rolling Stone</u> (the song, not the establishment rag)

Trump is the first President since Obama who would not permit a political enemy to retain his/her ambassadorship.

THEY TREATED HER LIKE A CHILD, BUT <u>YOU</u> ARE THE SEXISTS

Congressman: "Without upsetting you too much, how did it <u>feel</u> when you got fired?"

Yovanovitch: "I...I can't exactly say."

Imagine: "Mr. Ambassador, not to upset you too much, but how did it <u>feel</u>..."

Note: At least she didn't cry like Dr. Blasey Ford. Hear me Roar.

SO WHAT DOES THE ~~DISHWASHER~~ BUREAUCRAT <u>DO</u>?

Unelected gov-mint bureaucrats are now expected to countermand the wishes of our elected officials and to impose <u>their</u> will on foreign policy decisions.

Gillibrand Glossary: State Department Bureaucrat- Clocks in, then goes to breakfast. Chows down at a gov-mint subsidized cafeteria (paid for by YOU) at commissary prices & still steals his/her lunch in zip-lock bags. When the National Weather Service issues a snow alert for the District of Columbia and asks that "all non-essential gov-mint employees" stay home, they do.

HARD TO LISTEN WHEN YOU'RE TALKING

The job of a novice rider is to forget everything he did on the street, keep his mouth shut, and learn how to ride a motorcycle. The yuppie broad didn't get that memo. She interrupted the instructor needlessly and often; her track sessions were stupid-slow. Spying my 42-in drum fan in the pits (this was in July), she was incapable of walking by without a comment. "I have fan envy", she blabbed. "Is that all?", responded your peerless producer. Bitch finally shut the fuck up.

Editrix: But...but how did she _feel_?

NIKE ENDORSES COLIN KAEPERNICK

Sure it's backwards and real wrong. So is putting young Americans out of work by having your shit made in the Peoples Republic of Communist China at slave labor rates, then charging our kids top dollar. Nike sucks.

UNENDORSEMENT

DAP has the best salesmen in the world. These guys have gotten almost every hardware store in the Country to carry their company's crappy caulking.

THE THOUGHT OF REMOVING a President who was duly elected by the wrong people has Blitzer beaming and Lemon larking. You knew Day 1 went badly by their glumness. These DNC lackeys claimed "bombshell", but their faces said "bullshit".

RIGHT. SAFFRON, SKY & Phoenix should open their tofu & seeds shop on MLK Blvd and invite their lib-ral friends.

THEY REPRESENT US

Dragging our flag in the dirt while coarsely celebrating their victory was oddly unfulfilling, so the women's soccer team began shouting, "Lock up your wives!". The men's team has never been able to do that.

Q: Imply forced sex with married women?

A: Command that much testosterone.

SOCIALISTS ATTACK TRUMP'S NATIONALISM (AND YOUR STORE WINDOWS)

Mussolini had his Black Shirts, Hitler employed Brown Shirts, and Antifa thugs (CNN's "peaceful protesters") utilize the tactics of both.

Editrix: That is _so_ unfair! Hitler's National Socialists didn't hide their faces.

EINSTEIN'S THEORY OF RELATIVITY PROVEN

If you're hungry enough, you'll eat a Hot Pocket. Crust: 10% Red Army sox* (max)

Filling: (undetermined)

*They've been _washed_...

WE SEEM DOOMED TO REPEAT IT. THANK A TEACHER.

Today there are entire countries which could not stand up to one United States Navy aircraft carrier, just as whole nations often fell to one Roman legion. Nevertheless, after conquering and pacifying the western world, Rome came apart from within. The decay began the instant the gov-mint started putting its people on the dole. Sound familiar?

The latest spawn of democrat socialists, whose solution to everything is to use O.P.M.* to hand out "free" shit, need to study some history. Their NEA (union, no competency testing) teachers gave them no background, and the tenured hoaxes who infest our colleges have only revisionist crap to offer them. Fortunately, in this computer age, they can find out for themselves that what disintegrated the Roman Empire is about to do the same to US. *Other People's Money

For the religious: Rome's <u>sin</u> was its unbridled cruelty to people and animals. Ours is infanticide via late-term, partial birth, and now, post-partum murder of babies (doctor concurring, of course).

"But it's a women's health issue!" Bullshit. If baby can cry, it's murder.

P.S.: After they put the known world on welfare at the expense of a Country they despise (US), progressives would force the last working animals into state-sponsored retirement. A man in rural Vermont is routinely accosted by yuppie know-nothings when he exercises his mule in front of a properly-loaded cart. Nevermind that Mollie <u>lives</u> to pull the thing, stamping her feet to remind him when it's time to harness-up and go. Iditarod competitors get harassed by animal activists who somehow miss the smiles on the dogs' faces as they enthusiastically run pell-mell through the wilderness. Fire horses of yore would step out of their stalls and place themselves under the traces, "rarin' ta go". Vintage ox cart drivers see a similar willingness to work in their teams. It's what they were bred for; it's what they DO. No matter. Those who sit on their asses awaiting a gov-mint hand-out want everybody to do the same lest the workers make the slackers look like the parasites they are. Talkin' to <u>you</u>, Mollie.

BIN LADEN WAS KILLED because of Obama; Al Baghdadi got taken out in spite of Trump. CNN told me so.

HIGH MAINTENANCE

"No Standards" is a <u>joke</u>, Greg. (Hell, around here, it's a compliment.)

NAME RECOGNITION

President Trump met with a select* group of reporters yesterday. Included were Wolf Blitzer, Anderson Cooper, Dana Bash/Andrea Mitchell (it's the same chick), Ed Henry, Sean Hannity, Laura Ingraham, Tucker Carlson, Mark Levin, and Greg.

*"select" does not mean you have...standards.

I GOT YOUR LETTERS, FORREST

Q: How stupid are people who write letters?

A: So stupid that they know, they fucking <u>know</u>, that they'll get hacked on-line. These idiots pay their bills <u>by mail</u> to protect their identity. Swear to Greg.

HYGIENE

Lotsa ear wax removal machines on TV lately. Don't those people have car keys?

HE SHOT BAMBI'S MOM! -Disney Fake News (where CNN got its start)

A hunter knows that he is not eating meat from an animal that lived a life of misery on a factory farm. Do you?

P.S.: Hunting season opens after fawns are weaned and on their own.

OLD SCHOOL COOL VS NOT COOL

It's fun to ride a vintage bike, but put me on a Vincent, a Velocette, a BSA, Matchless, Norton, etc.; <u>anything</u> that doesn't have f-f-floorboards, f-f-fringe, and 95 reflectors on the back. Yes, and make it weigh less than a VW. Do-dah.

EDIBLE VENISON

We cling to it, but face it: deer meat tastes like... deer meat. Buddy o' mine overcomes this with biscuits of backstrap marinated in teriyaki and wrapped in bacon. I have lived inna South long enough to want to copycat this; unlike Country copying Rock*, I didn't wait 20-30 years to do so.

Luckily, he inadvertently included a tenderloin with the bambiburger he spent me home with. Fresh outta teriyaki 12 years ago, I countered with fitty-fitty soy sauce/balsalmic vinegar. A R in this stuff, plus coupla minutes onna greeil, and they was some fine cus-ween all 'round.

*Not just the riffs; the <u>antics</u>. Gee-tar man kickin' up his heels like a ijit. 40 (four-oh) year -old men with holes in they jeans (Swear to God) an' they hay-ir in ringlets (Swear to God). Gals in short, tight dresses and hooker heels...<u>its about time!</u>

NEVER TRUMP GUTLESSREPUBLICANS are now hanging on to the President's coattails.

THEE BABLE MEANS EVER word 'cept "wa-an', which ever-buddy knows is Hebrew for "gripe juice". -Deacon Earl

HEBREW HAPPY HOUR

Ancient Jewish ethics require one to feed his animals before himself. Thank Yahweh it does not include when one may commence his Cuba Libre. Gracias a Dios!

Note: Cuba Libre (the drink, not the movement) is the only socialist addition to the human endeavor that fucking works. <u>Somebody</u> tell Bernie.

PERSPECTIVE

"NFL jocks <u>earn</u> their exorbitant pay. On the field of play, they get hit." Soldiers should earn so much more. On the field of battle, they get shot.

REMEMBER HOME ECONOMICS? NEITHER DO I.

When you make a gallon of soup out of a turkey carcass, forget the noodles and put some stuffing, which by now is a tad crispy, into your bowl. Wow.*

*Welfare mavens may disregard: you threw out the LOs, since you didn't pay for the food inna first place. You have long since traded the pride of a paycheck for a handout. Be sure to thank your Democrat masters.

Confidential to Kammy: not all welfare mavens are black. Who is the racist here?

Warning: If you don't eat some cranberry sauce after this, your back breaks.

LIB-RAL LOGIC

Chic-fil-a's owners support family values and traditional marriage. They enable and encourage their employees, including those who are gay, to spend Sundays and holidays with their loved ones. These are hateful people.

LGBT-WHATEVERS support women's health issues, which of course is code for late-term and partial-birth abortion. Ably assisted by NEA (union, no competency testing) teachers in our gov-mint run school/child warehouse/indoctrination system, they encourage pre-teens to consider irreversible mutilation of their bodies on a puerile whim regardless the wishes of their stupid parents. (Misery craves company.) Like all obedient progressives, they want everybody on food stamps so, like them, we spend our grocery money on tattoos and piercings, acrylics and extensions, cigarettes, beer, blunts, and maybe even some rent money for Mom's basement. Dare to disagree and they will doxx you so masked Antifa thugs* can trample your lawn while terrorizing your family.**

*CNN calls them "peaceful protesters". So why the masks?

**LGBT-WTF consider families homophobic so they <u>deserve</u> to be terrorized.

These are lovely lads and lassies and whatevers. Ask any lib-ral.

MAN HAS SCREWED UP EVERY CHRISTIAN CHURCH, ESPECIALLY THE FIRST ONE*

"It is fitting indeed, and right, and just, our duty and our salvation, for us always and everywhere to give thanks." -Said at every Catholic Mass, everywhere in the world.

"Absolvo te." -I hope they still say that.

*ISLAM DIDN'T NEED ANY HELP: it started out stupid.

2020 DEMOCRAT PLATFORM, PLANK BY PLANK, BOARD BY (YAWN) BOARD.

Kamala Harris

"I usta jail everybody. Now I'll arrest no one. Make me your Chief Executive."

Pete Buttagieg

"I'm here, I'm queer. I have a husband. Make me your President/First Lady.

Elizabeth P. Fleming Warren

"Hey Moe! Let's import more people to give free shit to. Yeah, that's it!"

Bete O'Rourke

"I loathe myself and my white privilege. I should not have been born. Elect me."

Cory Booker

"I promise I'll behave in the White House bathroom."

THE NEW BULLY ON THE BLOCK

It was ambiguous at first, then plain but innocuous. Trust the LGBT-WHATEVERS to push it too far. Nobody wants to see two men sucking face on TV, or anyplace else for that matter. Ever. Americans are a tolerant people; all most of us ask is that you respect our privacy and keep your lurid lifestyle to yourselves.

American companies have now been pressured into airing ads that show same-sex couples as the norm. (Different-sex couples are OK if they are different races.) Have at it. Sales to 10% of the population will be brisk. The rest of us are tired of having the "progressive" lifestyle foisted on us; we will find other sources for our goods and services.

P.S.: Honest women admit that two (fem) chicks can be cute; two men: never. Two butch women: see "two men". Progressives may deny away, but that's just the way it is.

SEE HOUSES, STEP ON IT

Heavily-laden semi-trailer trucks, owned by companies half a continent away and driven by strangers, glide through town with nary a whisper. Local lumber trucks hammer in and out, their minimal mufflers roaring. Logging trucks lack any pretense of a functioning muffler, much as their drivers are devoid of a functioning hemisphere.

"But...but...jake brakes save clutches and brakes." Sure, Sparky; do does taking you foot out of it and coasting into town. Owner-operators do this, since their name is on the door and <u>they pay for the fuel</u>. Dumbass.

"But...but...we're the new American cowboys." Good thing you're not the old ones. Cattle have no kill switch, no brakes, and you have to be able to out-smart them.

In defense of dummies, GPS tracking now forces them to obey speed limits: no more making up time so they can hang out in a titty bar.* When you have the most boring job on the planet, you have to amuse yourself <u>somehow</u>. The Jacobs Brake has given you a way. Dumbass.

*No more "TOTAL NUDITY" signs on the Interstate for your kids to see. GPS has shut them down. Good. Dumbass.

WOMEN ARE SMARTER AND THEIR PRIORITIES ARE IN ORDER

The same broad who would divorce you for losing a lid will shriek, "That's not <u>Tupperware</u>! Throw it out!"

They, like, know the difference.

P.S.: Meant to say "person". We're LGBT-WHATEVER friendly 'round here.

NOTE TO 'STEEMED PUBLISHER: Muse, schmooze; shit like this happens when I drink my lunch.

THEY CHOOSE*, YOU LOSE

Hate Speech: anything you say about lib-rals.
Free Speech: <u>anything</u> lib-rals say about you.
* in the other lib-ral "choice", somebody dies.
Glossary

Conservative: rips babies from invading illegal alien mother's arms and nurses them both back to health.

democratic socialist: rips babies from mother's womb and kills them.
communist: does same, but only to female babies.
feminist: ignores all of the above.
lib-ral: ignores all of the above; sings "Cumbaya".

Catholic Charities: stows unvetted, undocumented, unemployed illegal alien invaders among working folk who are too busy to notice until it is too late, far, far away from the bishopric, but only after forcing them to sing "Cumbaya".

Democrat presidential candidate: pretends he/she/it does not know what partial-birth abortion is; opposes freedom of choice for school vouchers. Cumbaya.

Morality: allow the entire jobless World into your Country when feelin' good; kill your viable baby when feelin' icky. Fucking cumbaya.

IF YOU LIKED TAWANA BRAWLEY, YOU'LL **LOVE** JUSSIE SMOLLET

Every* Democrat presidential candidate, male, female and undecided, scurried into the National Action Network Victimhood Conference to kiss Al (The Reverend) Sharpton's ass. Voting for any of them in 2020 condones this collection of cockroaches. Yay.

*'Cept Joe (out getting some head)

LAURA: "WOMEN ARE LUMBERJACKS."
  Lib-ral: "They shouldn't appropriate a toxicmasculine name."
  Phil Berto: "Aw, just call 'em 'lumberjanes' to sidestep penis envy."
  Any Feminist: "Buzzz...Zaappp!"
  Cool.
  P(m)S: Hide the saws & axes 5 days a month.
  Q: What would ladies **do**?
  A: The dishes.

K.M.D., C.P.A.: "WELL, you <u>do</u> have a strong personality." Translation: "Well, you <u>are</u> a pain in the ass.

PLAIN PLANE GEOMETRY: THE OBTUSE ANGLE* (WHO IS THE RACIST HERE?)
  I was throwin' Cheetos at the TV screen, willing Laura Ingraham and/or her guest, Reagan biographer Craig Shirley, to say, "Att AOC: Reagan never supposed that all welfare queens are black; <u>you</u> did". But they didn't.
  *sorry.

THE KKK, THE GREAT SOCIETY, SOCIALISM
  Democrat whims are all over the place. The Conservative* ideal is as constant as it is compelling: equal opportunity to <u>work</u> to better yourself and prosper, unencumbered by phony philanthropy for parasites who live on hand-outs.

  *Almost said "Republican", but many are gutless wonders who don't support their own President.

FEMINISM HAS TRIUMPHED
  Swiffer ads always feature men; women don't know what it is.
  Q: When is a man allowed to drive in a car/truck ad?

A: When his wife's name is "Bruce".

TOO EASY

President Trump ended Elizabeth Fleming Warren's candidacy with one word.

IT IS FINISHED

Q: Would you sew up my jeans, Gramma?

A: "Sew"? What's "sew"? Now hand me my hash pipe and go play in the street.

Gramma's parents fought a World War; Dad on the front lines, Mom expertly* building weapons of war. Parenting skills suffered; their kids obliged by turning on, dropping out, and "walking in" their dungarees. Yep, they dragged their clothing over spit-on sidewalks 'till the heels of their Frye boots wore the hem to length. Morons. Factor in iron-on patches, and sewing skills went they way of child rearing**. NOTE: Aging hippies taught their kids very little, so not much was left to pass on, making today's numbskulls easy prey for NEA (union, no competency testing) teachers/socialist indoctrinators. It's <u>over</u>.

> *A heavy bomber's four 27-cylinder radial engines had 140 connections that could leak oil. They didn't.

> ** So-called due to the epicenter of spanking/belting/switching. Look it up.

THANK ANY LIBERAL

Q: What do you now call a parent who spanks a child?

A: A felon.

THE PRESIDENT SHOULD release his tax returns when Congress does likewise.

####### RESISTANCE ##### RESISTANCE ##### RESISTANCE ##### RESISTANCE ######

"STUDENTS": Join the Resistance. Express an original thought in the presence of your paid professional liberal indoctrinator a/k/a NEA (union, no competency testing) teacher, then enjoy your suspension. You will learn far more at the beach or in the mountains, even if you just enjoy the scenery. Lose the phone and read <u>Animal Farm</u> by George Orwell. Upon your return, try not to laugh when your learned professor tries to tell you a damn thing. Freedom!

YUPPIES <u>NEED</u> DESIGNER WASHER/DRYERS IN THEIR RENTAL APARTMENTS

Problem: A square white $300 ($150 scratch & dent) machine will launder the bejesus outta your clothes and last 20-30 years if bitch doesn't crazy-overload it. The water it uses is never lost, the Earth being a closed system. So, how can we fuck this up?

Solution: Hire coupla housewife-engineers who never heard of "form follows function" to build a designer-styled contraption that proports to wash a week's worth of clothing (plus two sheets and a comforter that some aging hippie broad sneaks in) with a quart of water*. Give it electronic controls, since these things are never placed where there could possibly be dampness, insects, children, etc.

*So, it's the least you could do since that bastard Trump pulled us out of the Paris Accord, which would have saved .01°F of global warming over the next 100 years (we think) with the U.S.A. contributing 90% of the $20 billion thrown down the drain each and every year. So, can I get a cumbaya?

HOLD A GRUDGE

Morton. The folks who gave us pot pies with no bottom crust also sold a "lemon" pie that contained no lemon. "Better living through chemistry."

Pacific Coast Highway (P.C.H.). Purveyors of trendy bathing suits with "brass washed" **steel** buttons. (You think I am making this up, don't you?)

All major U.S. coffee companies used anything but arabica beans to save a penny a pound until a more informed public knew better.

The worst, of course, is Mueller's. For most of my lifetime they marketed pasta products labelled "Semolina **plus** Farina" until better-educated consumers (finally) realized it was like saying "Semolina **plus** Sawdust". Their stuff is now 100% semolina wheat, but only because they were caught. Hold a grudge.

Q: WHEN WILL THE UNVETTEDILLEGALALIENINVADERS who have been hidden among us by the Archbishopric be housed in His Excellency's own subdivision?

A: Soon, Ralph. Soon.

Onna plus side, whenever their charges demand and get "free" (taxpayer-funded) medical care, steal a car, burglarize a home, or destroy a $50,000 irrigation system to rip out $50 worth of copper, why, Catholic Charities will make full restitution.....just kidding.

BACHELOR TIP: TURNING on the kitchen ceiling fan for the first time in months sure thickens the soup.

DEMOCRAT PLATFORM

Legal immigrants may vote Republican. Illegal immigrants <u>will</u> vote Democrat. Do-dah.

THE NATIONAL ACTION NETWORK vs FREEDOM OF CHOICE

It is now impossible to choose the Democrat ticket without voting for someone who kissed Al Sharpton's ass.

LIB-RAL VS FREEDOM OF CHOICE

If you want to know what America will be like under "liberal" rule, wear a (blank) red hat on any college campus.

BUT...BUT...IT HAS MEDICAL USES

I have never known a weedhead who was an overachiever, and neither have you. Habitual potheads <u>define</u> those who never, ever have their shit together.

FOXUNWORTHY

You might could be a moron if you have $100 worth of junk in the garage and a $40,000 vehicle in the driveway.

WHEN FALSE IS TRUE AND TRUE IS...FAKE

Fox News: There were 100,000 arrests at the border last month.

Democrat: Your figures are inaccurate. Some invaders turned themselves in.

NOTE: Fox News should have said, "99,998 arrests were made last month, plus the two illegals who turned themselves in". CNN, of course, would have said, "Over a thousand arrests..."

CNN has this shit <u>down</u>. When 300,000 Moms for Infanticide marched on D.C., CNN called it the "Million Mom March". When 300,000 Right to Life Folks demonstrated, CNN reported "over 1,000". True but fake. Do-dah.

SOCIALISM 101

A cough syrup/expectorant sold for $16. Free market capitalism stepped in, added a decongestant, and now offers it at Family Dollar for $2.50.

Q: Do you really want the gov-mint to fuck that up?

A: I am a Democrat, so, why, yes. Yes I do. Here's how.

Gov-mint will form a Committee to look into this. Three years and $3 million later, they will set up ('nother year, 'nother $1 million) a Department. They will try to force a matching price, but settle for $3. Add $1 for the petty bureaucrat's salary & benefits, $2 for his/her/its* Supervisor's salary & benefits, $3 for the Department Head's salary & benefits, and $4 to incentivize a compliant congressperson to sponsor the requisite legislation. Tack on a 30% margin of error and, why, you're back up to $16...well, $16.90, actually.

*We're LGBT-WHATEVER friendly 'round here.

LIBERAL LOGIC, MILITANT MATH

At least one baby has been accidentally shot. I am certain of it. Meanwhile, millions have been murdered after they were developed enough to cry courtesy of late-term, partial-birth, and now, after-birth abortion. Guess which one a million moms marched against?

At CNN, 300,000 gun "control" folks equals "one million".

At CNN, 300,000 right to life people equals "over 1,000".

Q: Fake news?

A: Do-dah.

WHO ELECTS THESE PEOPLE?

"Unjust laws" imprisoned the Boston Marathon bomber. -Democrat Congressperson

<u>I agree with her</u>. He should have been taken out and shot.

P.S.: Why, next we'll have Democrat presidential candidates championing the right of rapists, child molesters, and murderers to vote...Oops!

REPARATIONS

White Americans freed American slaves during the Civil War. "Reparations" were paid in blood, North and South. You're welcome.

PATRIARCHY IS PASSE'

Woman: a being, some say sentient, who buys shirts with buttons in the back*, sacrifices the vision of one eye for a <u>hairstyle</u>**, hangs shiny objects from her rear-view mirror***, and hits stationary objects because she "never drove that car before"****.

*Swear to God.

**You think I am making this up, don't you?

***Aw, to be blinded by glare you'd have to **look** at it.

****It had no fuzzy thing on the steering wheel.

NOTE: No man ever bought size 7 shoes for his size 8 feet.

EQUAL RIGHTS SECTION

Watch for our toxic masculinity missives, which will be petulantly proffered five days out of each and every month.

GALA ILLEGALALIENJOBLESSINVADER SECTION

Q: Do you want to give your Country away to the entire third world?
A: I am Democrat, so yes, yes I do.
Q: Will you give up part of your paycheck to support strangers?
A: I am a Democrat, so yes, yes I will give up part of your paycheck.

I LOVED DATING A SCHOOLTEACHER. She corrected my grammar, my manners, and said, "Do that over again, Mister!"

GRANDE DAME VS UNWORTHY BUREAUCRATS

Church fires are tough. When a massive cathedral is ablaze, things get real crazy real fast. Factor in millennium-old original growth lumber that has resided under a sheet lead roof for 8 centuries, well, those rafters were a tad dry. Folks who wonder why some fire streams were not directed at the source of the flames should know that, once the roof was a goner, the best use of those streams was to protect the as-yet unburned portions of the building (the "exposures"). The survival of the bell towers and main walls attests to the success of this tactic.

As usual, mistakes were made, at about 10% the rate of every other field of human endeavor. As always, there was no lack of courage, as firefighters and civilians ventured where huge burning timbers fell from 120' aloft to save precious art and artifacts.

> NOTE: Capitalism has provided St. Patrick's Cathedral with state of the art fire prevention/suppression systems. Socialism was scared to do likewise <u>for a national symbol</u> because it has religious connections. Fortunately, many concerned capitalists have stepped up to assist with the restoration at a thousand times what prevention would have cost.

> P.S.: Several socialist have offered to visit the site as a show of solidarity, but only if gov-mint pays their expenses.

CIRCLING THE BOWL

The Democrat operatives masquerading as reporters at CNN were glum. They knew that AG Barr was about to flush the collusion toilet they had been swilling in for 2 1/2 years. He did.

NOTE: Part of their patter was to implement their ability to read his mind and declare that Trump would invoke executive privilege. He didn't.

THAT...THAT PENIS THING. AGAIN.

FEMINISTS WHO DENY any difference in the abilities of the sexes should try to leave the house without their purses.

PURSES & PRICKS

Awaiting AG Barr's arrival, they treated us to a dissertation on The Complete History of Executive Privilege: It's Pros & Cons. Even as the axe was about to fall, CNN's Democrat lackeys stepped on their own dicks* once again. Once again, Trump dumped them. Cool.

> * 'Cept the ladies. CNN's women can't step on 'em, 'counta they carry them in their...purses.

> Q: Is this fake news?
> A: This is fake dick.

DATING AN OPTOMETRIST WAS COOL. She'd say, "Is it better like this, or better like this?".

DEMOCRAT PLATFORM

Health care. Opioid epidemic. Veterans affairs. Border crisis. Social Security insolvency. National debt. Upside-down trade agreements.

Q: You guys gonna fix all that?

A: No, silly; we're gonna ignore all that and concentrate on hectoring a duly-elected president.

COMIN' AND GOIN'

Cat food companies also make kitty litter. Sure, it's a soft market, but it hardly seems fair.

SHELF SPACE

Cat litter companies don't combine good features. This one has 24-hour odor control, that one acts instantly. Picture some pinch-faced yuppie broad shrieking, "I want low-tracking litter. Don't you dare give me that odor control stuff!"

NOTE: the above explains why half the Democrat Party thinks it would be a Good Idea to adopt the economic system of Venezuela.

TWITTER TALLY

Alexandria Ocasio Cortez tweets on:

...............Mosque attack: 14

...............Church bombing: 0

.......Synagogue shooting: -6

Update: Poway perp not Muslim; AOC issues Shouldn't Shoot Up Synagogues screed.

WHEN DID "SOCIAL JUSTICE" BECOME SYNONYMOUS WITH HAND-OUTS?

Helping a stranger in need is one thing, but Christianity never suggested providing a free ride for deadbeats on the backs of working folks. Even St. Paul is clear: no work, no eat. Communism closed churches because they taught the ultimate social justice: doing your fair share and contributing <u>something</u> to the community, and the dignity of work.

NOTE: Communism's wimpy twin, socialism, is sneakier; it silently subverts scripture* via socialist prelates who have forgotten that free-market capitalism <u>pays the bills</u>. These dudes are gonna take a serious cut in salary when socialism turns the planet into one third-world hellhole. Amen.

*Three generations of NEA (union, no competency testing) liberal teachers have set today's youngsters up for failure to see the danger.

CULTURAL ENRICHMENT

I asked the Archbishopric if promoting diversity included replacing bingo with cock fighting. I received no reply. Maybe they no speaka...

A DEMOCRAT'S DREAM: "Hi, my name is Pete, I have a husband, and I'm running for President."

WHY WE TRAIN THEM

Think aging Fido is being froward? So did I. Turns out he's deaf* as a post and no longer trusts his legs. Be glad you taught him hand signals. Now loop a wide belt under his belly to provide a little lift (and confidence) to get him up the stairs.

*Yuppies: this means "hearing impaired" with 11 fewer letters. Look it up.

IF ONLY HILLARY...WASN'T A JERK

Trump has little to fear in 2020. Democrats will still be talking about 2016.

KAMMY KICKS THE CAN (IT'S WHAT ESTABLISHMENT POLITI-CIANS DO)

Reporter: Do you think that convicted terrorists should vote?

United States Senator Harris: "We could have a conversation about that..."

Bro, I <u>like</u> it!

Po-lice: Is that your open container/weed/meth in the center console?

"Disabled" (wink, wink): "We could have a conversation about that..."

Insurance agent: Is that your Volvo/Saab/Prius/Beemer/VW bus in that tree?

Sky L. lib-ral: "We could have a conversation about that..."

E.R. Doctor: Is that your remote-controlled dildo up his/her/its/whatever's ass?

His/her/its/whatever's "husband": "We could have a conversation about that..."

E.R. Nurse: Could you at least turn it off?

Lib-rals: I said "nurse", you thought "female". Who is the sexist here?

*Which is why Trump scares the crap outta 'em.

A MOST PECULIAR MAN

He had no friends, he seldom spoke-

And no one in turn ever spoke to him,

'Cause he wasn't friendly, and he didn't care,

<u>And he wasn't like them</u>...

-Paul Simon

LIB-RAL "FREE" (ON THE BACKS OF WORKERS) SUMMER VACATION

1. Sneak into any socialist country. Take coupla kids.
2. Have no job prospects.
3. In your language, not theirs, demand food, shelter and medical care.
4. Put the kids in public school.
5. Sign up for every taxpayer-funded benefit you can find.

6. Call me from prison.

NOTE: Avoid the above! Sneak into Maryland and fucking **vote** in local elections. You paid sales tax on your tattoos, piercings, cigarettes & cerveza, so food stamps are a given. De nada.

OMAR

"America was built on the backs of slaves." Dang. Didn't <u>any</u> of those white people work?

REVIEW

IT IS THE MOST LOW-key "war movie" I have seen. Strongly based on fact, it portrays the remnants of a beaten army trying to stay alive, often via less than heroic means. Even the signature RAF fighter pilot is mild-mannered in his bravery; there is no spirit of derring-do, no "top gun" hotdogging. He could re-cross the Channel to safety on his remaining 5 gallons of fuel; he quietly decides to expend his last pound of petrol protecting the Tommies who are being shot up on the beaches. No matter. The movie critics, always whores to social fads, lacked the balls to pan this fine film, so they simply ignored it rather than buck the most powerful hate group* of our time: radical feminists. Calling the movie "a monument to maleness" (maleness = malignity), the harridans were incensed that it failed to pretend that women took part in the fighting.

NOTE: A documentary about the sinking of the USS Indianapolis proved that one may no longer say that 300 men were saved and 800 men were blown to bits, burned to death, drowned, or eaten by sharks. One must call them "persons".

Anyway, <u>Dunkirk</u> has pissed off all the right persons. We highly recommend it.

*Al Sharpton and Jesse Jackson do not peddle hate groups. These "reverends" (gimme a break) are victimization hustlers. Do-dah.

P.S.: Trannies are now vying for virulence with the leslies. Girl Power. Yay.

END GLOBAL WARMING: STOP BREEDING*

The same cumbaya crowd which decried overpopulation now wants open borders. It seems that brown overpopulation is better than white overpopulation.

NOTE: Brown **must** be better. Legendary Latino animal abuse (bullfights, cockfights, dog fights, taking undersize fish, ripping <u>both</u> claws off fiddler crabs which then starve to death, being culturally incapable of spaying/neutering a pet, etc.) draws not a peep from PETA. Latino laceration of the landscape springs silence from The Sierra Club. Rampant reef raping garners Greenpeace nescience. PC is now brown blind. Ole!

CRAPPY SINGER

Always the avant-garde one, second Sis bought one of the first Johnny Mathis records ever pressed. Dad was unimpressed. In a chilling portend of things to come, Sis got the entire family on-board with, "Aw, you just hate him because he's black". Ignoring the canard, Dad quietly replied, "He sings like a girl". Now, didn't **I** feel like a fucking asshole.

REALLY CRAPPY SINGER

Don't hear much from Sheryl Crow anymore. I guess her family quit buying her records.

REALLY CRAPPY PRESIDENT*

"Aw, you just hate him because he's black." I can picture Dad saying, "Well then. I guess I only half hate him".

*Jimmy Carter is sooo relieved.

DUNKIRK REVISITED

Only a smattering of RAF forces were dispatched to defend the Dunkirk troop evacuation to avoid risking planes & pilots needed to defend against an invasion. (I hope) I would have sent the whole shebang. I believe that an overwhelming response would have lost fewer planes, not more, while serving notice (**Achtung!**) that an attack against British forces, anywhere, would be met with annihilation. Moreover, any Kraut killed at Dunkirk would be one less to deal with later.

Afterward, the sorry sumbitch* who apologized for our actions* would be put on community organization for the duration.

*Talkin' 'bout Neville Chamberlain here. What were **you** thinking, you lib-ral yuppie racist bastard?

Q: Post-Obama, can a tachometer still have a redline?

A: So, not on campus.*

*too divisive

P.S.: Ask any girl what a tach is; the boys are playin' Dungeons and & Dragons. It Takes A Village.

JOB INSECURITY POST COLLUSION

Wolf. Dana. Anderson. Andrea. Lookit their faces: stoic, almost sheepish. They know, **they fucking know**, that they have been feeding you a line of zuckershit. <u>They have no choice</u>. After the hoax of the century, their only other job prospect is flippin' burgers at Micky D's...unless...maybe they can find someone who destroyed 30,000 E-mails. Do-dah.

> **Note:** Aw, that's ridiculous. There would have to be hammer-smashed phones, acid –washed hard drives, $500,000 "speaking fees", $1,000,000 "donations", uranium sold to Russia, etc. Who would **do** that?

AH, THE SANCTITY OF MOTHERHOOD...

Buncha Moms <u>had to be told</u> how NOT to dress when coming on campus to discharge/pick up their spawn. High marks to the Principal, but what chance have the kids?

SHELTERED

Democrat front runner: "We went into the 'hood. Really. Spoke with some women of color." Yeah, Joe. They're out there.

> **Note:** Sure, Biden mentioned "black" and "women", but he forgot to crowbar "gay", "lesbian", "still not sure", and "Hispanic cross-dressers for saving the Planet" into the conversation. What Democrat will vote for him? NEXT: Joe visits a 7-11 to see some Pakis.

Q: Why so hard on someone who is fading fast?
A: He's a liar and, now, an ijit.

THE REAL FREEDOM OF CHOICE

See your friends & neighbors at the local auto parts store or call Rock Auto and get a yuppie geek who has never <u>seen</u> your ride. Duh.

BORDER NO CRISIS: DEMS DO THEIR PART

Stop by Pelosi's Palace or Kammy's Kompound for a free glass of water. Limit 1. <u>No taxpayers</u>. Hablamos Espanol.

MORE YUPPIE BULLSHIT

Lifelock routinely sends me "last chance" enrollment cards marked **Lifelock Official Welcome Kit.** Swear to God. Now there's yet another way for my credit information to be stolen.

> **Note:** Yuppies <u>need</u> shit like Lifelock 'cause they're stupid. They voted for Hillary, didn't they? Plus, they "save paper" by paying bills online (Gee, d'ya think someone'll hack this?) and then get a statement says "This page intentionally left blank". Dumbass.

> **P.S.:** To (try to) Make It Stop, contact Brendan McFarlin, "Director of Member Experience" (You think I am making this up, don't you?). Like I said: more yuppie bullshit.

ATT OMAR AND PELOSI

You hate this Country, oblivious to the fact that no Nation ever wielded so much power with so much restraint. Please confine yourselves to your native socialist hellholes (Somalia and San Francisco) until you know something.

FLORIDA/GEORGIA LINE

Think you'll beat the lunch hour rush at the liquor store by showing up at opening time? Pshaw! They'll be lined up at the door, jonesing for they julep.

P.S.: Thee Methodists wheel speak to you; thee Baptists wheel not.

YA GOTTA HAVE RULES

For 8 years, Obama's self-described "wingman", United States Attorney General Eric Corrupt Holder, weaponized the Justice Department against

Haplessrepublicans. Now that collusion is kaput, Democrats are accusing Trump's "hand-picked" AG of doing likewise to them.

Q: D'ya think they read Saul Alinsky's <u>Rules For Radicals</u>?

A: Who has time? They read Hillary's college paper on her hero.

*Somebody tell our liberal-compliant "news" media that <u>all</u> AGs are "picked".

THE PLUS SIDE TO LOSING AN ANIMAL

Their suffering is over AND you have one more angel lookin' out for you.

FEMALE AGGRESSION: A TALE OF TWO THEORIES

1- **Replacement.** When Dad-less boys are non-reared by minimum-wage day care underachievers (thank any feminist), then get brainwashed by lib-ral teachers, they end up playing Mortal Kombat while the girls step up and get shit done.

2- **Compensation.** Everybody knows that slow-kill (suffocation/starvation) baby animal traps a/k/a Yoplait Yogurt backwards containers are cutsey-designed to please the female psyche*. They try to hide this fact with aggression. Proof? Call any feminist "cute". **Note:** She'll still go "Awww..." at footage of stuck skunks, squirrels, opossums, etc. PETA? Greenpeace? Anyone? Anyone?

*unencumbered by logic

DARWIN GOT IT WRONG: IT'S GOING THE OTHER WAY.

Man cannot text and drive; lovebugs can fuck and <u>fly</u>.

ARCING FOR AN ANGLE: PERMANENT FIRST MULLET vs MARLIN

10 Michelle Obama fashion magazine covers vs. 10 Melania Trump missed opportunities. Theme music: Eurasian Eyes by Corey Hart.

> P.S.: Yuppie broads in baseball caps look like yuppie broads in baseball caps. Melania (and now, Laura Ingraham), similarly hatted and absent the (usually requisite) hair framing, present impeccable, classic beauty. Yes, it would be cheeky to make it a 3-way comparison, but a man can dream...

GENDER ID MADE EASY

At any college commencement, the graduates who immediately move their tassels right to left are genetic males. Hesitation/confusion/looking around to see what everybody else does: chick. Do-dah.

MORE ANDROGYNY

Says "north", "south", "east", "west", "left", "right": dude.
Says "toward Saks" and runs ceiling fans backwards: it's a broad.

THEY SUFFER SILENTLY (P.S.: IF YOU HAVE ORDERED "SCALLOPS", YOU HAVE EATEN SKATE)

Asked Unified Sportsmen of Florida to sponsor legislation to outlaw shark finning in Florida waters. They said it is not their thing. NRA bureaucrats ignored the same suggestion. One would think they'd want the positive publicity. Gonna send it to our new Governor. If Mr. DeSantis ever considers higher office (I hope he does), he should jump on it now and expand it to US territorial waters later. Also needed is a heavy fine for cutting the tail off a stingray or skate. Bro, if you are so ill-equipped that you lack pliers and gloves, cut the line. Cost you a 10¢ hook, which the fish will work out in coupla days. Dumbass.

"What you do for (to) the least of these, you do for (to) Me."

You have head of this, no? 'Course, fundamentalists will argue that (to) is not biblically correct based on their intimate knowledge of Aramaic, Greek, Hebrew, and Latin and nevermind that they demonstrate linguistic flexibility when claiming that biblical wine was actually grape juice. Amen.

Q: How did the ancients preserve grape juice?

A: Wine.

Suggestion: Try following the spirit of the sermon rather than the letter of the law. Jesus already fired the Pharisees.

DOUCHEBAG DEFINED BY A MAN WHO HAS NEVER SEEN ONE

Just what the Catholic Church needs: 'nother priest/embarrassment. Chicago's own Father Pflager hosted Louis Farrakan but forgot to affect his fake black accent. Att Pope Francis: nihil obstat calling this asshole into your office and telling him to shut the fuck up.

NUMBER OF "GOOD" MUSLIMS WHO HAVE CONDEMNED THROWING QUEERS OFF BUILDINGS: -6

CNN TAKE NOTE

'When you have to advocate on behalf of a constitutional crisis, there isn't one.

-Ari Fleischer

GALA AWARDS SECTION

When better fake news is aired, CNN will air it.

Honorable mention: CBS, NBC, ABC, MSNBC, (taxpayer-funded) PBS

HE WANT'S <u>WHAT</u>? AND HE'LL <u>PAY</u> FOR IT?

Pennsylvania State Democrat Congressperson Brian Sims will pay you $100 for the address of a teenage girl. He should get his own (adult) action, or stick with Rosie Palm. Pervert. P.S.: Says he wanted the info for political reasons. I believe him. Sims & Father Pflager are a couple.

DEMS DON'T WANT NO MORE WHITE CANDIDATES. <u>I UNDER-STAND</u>.

"Onliest way we'd let Barack in is if'n he brung our coffee." –Bill & Hill

"I have met Obama. He's intelligent, polite, and he's <u>clean</u>." –Sleepy Joe

More recently, the Democrat front-runner went "Into the 'hood. <u>Really</u>." To see some black people. (Yes, Joe, they're out there.)

Q: Were they clean?

A: And so...well-spoken. <u>Really</u>.

Q: Is this the best the Dems have?

A: <u>Really</u>.

NOTE: Suddenly, our modern-day (deplorable) "Davy Crockett Goes To Washington"* redeaux makes sense. Lotsa sense. (Bureaucrats hated Davy, too.)

*vintage Disney production (irony)

GUTLESS (IN YUPPIESPEAK)

They are quick to condemn those who oppose same-sex "marriage".

Q: So, why don't lib-rals ask Muslims not to kill homosexuals?

A: So, because they are afraid of them?

Q: So, why don't "good" Muslims ask Muslims not to kill homosexuals?

A: So, because they are afraid of them?

Q: So, why don't Democrat candidates ask Muslims not to kill homosexuals?

A: So, because they **are** them?

Q: So, are they Muslim or homosexual?
A: Yes.

MULCH: <u>DEFINES</u> PREVENTING GROWTH. MULCHING LAWN-MOWER: <u>DEFINES</u> STUPIDITY.

Borrow a bagging mower. Produce a mound of lawn waste you can hide behind. Spread that pile of weed seeds & stems over your lawn and act surprised when fungus and fennel take over. Dumbass.

> **Plan B:** Blow all that shit out into the street (Don't <u>that</u> make the job look "finished"), then act surprised (again) when the storm drain backs up and your house floods. Dumbass.

PERSONAL TO HILLARY: You call me and mine "deplorable", but I'm over it.

A MAN EATING LION ESCAPED from a zoo and sought refuge on a college campus. It starved to death.

AMERICAN JURISPRUDENCE TURNED EXACTLY BACKWARDS

"I cannot indict; neither can I exonerate." –Special Prosecutor Robert Mueller

Bob. Buddy. It is not your job to exonerate anybody. Presumption of innocence handles that. You have heard of this, no?

DIVERSITY NOW MEANS SKIN COLOR **<u>ONLY</u>**

If you doubt the wisdom of the electoral college, consider today's mob tyranny of political correctness, shouting down speakers who dare to demonstrate diversity of thought, and absolute control of the establishment broadcast and print media by the left. Those old dead white men saw it coming. You're welcome.

LIAR!

Maestro Trump ended Elizabeth Fleming Warren's candidacy with one word.*

*Beto will be tougher: "Plays with do-do".

DOLLARS & SENSE (WE DEMAND EQUALITY! GIMMME YOUR CREDIT CARD.)

"Hon, please pick up the pizza. Get yourself some spending money, too."

A nice girl draws the cash and buys the pizza.

A smart girl charges the pizza, <u>then</u> hits the ATM.

Never, ever date a smart girl.

DEMOCRAT THINK TANK

Moe: We must end global warming.

Larry: We'll start by killing capitalism, which pays the bills.

Curley: When the Earth is all one third-world hellhole, fossil fuels use will be replaced by (recycled) dung fires, and we'll drink creek water that we bathe in after we dump our garbage in it. Yeah, that's it!

Q: There'll be no more cows, so the dung'll be...

A: Yep.

THEY STICK TOGETHER

Dale asked to stop by the Foodway for a box of pontoons. I wondered why she grabbed a shopping cart until I watched her do 50 bucks worth of grocery shopping in 90 seconds. At the counter, her best dangerous smile prompted me to drag out a C-note and pay the bill. As if I had never existed, the female cashier hands Dale the change and says, "Thank you". To Dale, not to me; I had already become invisible. The clutch purse maw was already open. "We'll just put this in here", says Mistress Dale, and at the closing click I knew that's where it was gonna stay. All eyes (chicks included) were on her too-tight, too-short skirt and her 4 and 9/16-inch (measured 'em) sparkly high heels as I followed her like any puppy dog out to the car. Sometimes ya gotta get off your wallet and just enjoy the view.

P.S.: I hope Dale never accepts the demotion to "equality".

TEST YOURSELF: "MICROWAVE for 110, 220, 330, etc., seconds." If you press 111, 222, 333, etc,. you pass.

GOOD LUCK IN PRISON –Sir John Gielguld, <u>Arthur</u>

The only reason that the former heads of the CIA, FBI, and other Deep State bureaucracies are pulling so many dirty tricks to discredit Trump and Barr is that they know, they fucking **know**, that when Trump is re-elected, lotsa them are going to jail.

TRYIN' TO IMPRESS HER

Think of all the jack you've spent on flowers (Pshaw!), perfume (tee-hee.), Charles Jourdan...well, OK, Rack Room shoes. Did it change your life? Didn't think so. Bro, I've seen the ads, and so have you. If'n you really want to see her eyes roll back in her head, buy her a Hershey Bar. You'll Get It Done and save enough to (finally) get your Kimber Custom Shop .45. Do-dah.

MUCK TV

<u>**Teen Mom**</u>. Yeah, that's it! Idealize undeveloped bags of hormones that re-produce themselves. But windmill farms will save the planet. Gimme a break.

May we suggest a counterpoint show: <u>Teen Tubes Tied Before They Breed And Spawn More Morons</u>. MTV won't touch it: too "judgmental"*. Let's ask Fox; common sense still exists there.

*The left has fashioned "judgmental" into a Bad Word (tsk, tsk).

~~God~~ Earth Mother forbid we exercise some judgment in our conduct.

P.S.: Today's teenage boys are useless, but teenage girls are <u>scary</u>.

('Course, I'd rather be scary than useless.)

I WONDER IF THEY'LL USE NEA (UNION, NO COMPETENCY TESTING) TEACHERS

Your Gov-mint now wants to teach jobless indigent illegal alien invaders to speak English. They have given up on your kids.

1- Girls now join Boy Scouts. (You think I am making this up, don't you?) I'll give you $100 (no, not for a girl's address: that's Brian Sims' job) for every Rio Grande Swim Team member who doesn't know "nino" from "nina".

2- A Delta Team risked life &limb to rescue a 90lb. soldierette who was captured during the Iraq War. The tyke tiffled*, "I only joined the Army to get a degree so I could teach kindergarten". (You think I am making this up...) Apparently the whole A-R-M-Y thing confused her. Thank a teacher.

NOTE: FailingIrrelevantTime Magazine described her as "waiflike". Hey Moe! That's it! Let's confront our enemies with an army of waifs!

EDITOR: Not so fast. We <u>could</u> field a battalion of bloated butches, give them bad haircuts, tell them they're fat, arm them with SUVs...

***tiffle:** talk while (petulantly) sniffling/sniveling (Look it up)

BUSY DOING...SOMETHING: Yes, the cat knows his name; he just wishes you wouldn't use it so much.

YOU WORK TO FEED YOUR FAMILY, BUT <u>I WANT NEW EAR-RINGS</u>!

Hollywood movies (Arthur, Garden State, etc.) often wink at shoplifting. No surprise there: so many petty thieves-turned-thespians inhabit the place. I wonder if Lindsey Lohan's bartenders tilt the tabs, or if Barbara Streisand hangs <u>her</u> laundry on a rope?

<u>FINALLY</u>, FISCAL RESPONSIBILITY FROM A DEMOCRAT

Pete Buttigieg has a husband. (You think I am making this up, don't you?) If elected, he will be President <u>and</u> First Lady. Secret Service Staff can then be cut in half. Yay.

FAMILY DOLLAR$ AND NO ¢ENSE

The shelves holding 40 facings of Clorox 6% sodium hypochlorite and water are always full. The shelves holding 20 facings of store brand 6% sodium hypochlorite and water are always empty. (Am I going too fast for you?) The American consumer (finally) Gets It. Some day the store owner ~~will~~ may.

P.S.: Cat litter, evaporated milk, chocolate mini-donuts: never.

Note: Scented and "bargain" bleaches are not required to list the percentage of "inactive ingredient" (water). So they don't. Shalom Bleach Company (Swear to God), Boca Raton, Florida (Swear to God): "We are not required to list it on the label". OK, so <u>tell</u> me. "We are not required to tell you." Oy, vey! Guess how much Shalom Bleach we bought after <u>that</u>.

POCAHONTAS*

Denying her white privilege, Elizabeth Fleming Warren refused to use her wealth and family connections to crowbar her way into Cornell (Or was it the other way Ivy League school, Yale?). Nope, she went all politically correct, claimed she was Native American, and screwed an Indian** outta a job.

* "Name fit like shit between toe." –any Jamaican

    * PC Alert: When his train was attacked by pissed-off Pawnee, W.C. Fields knocked one out with a booze bottle. "I forgot that it's illegal to split a bottle with an Indian", intoned Fields. We now know he should have said, "Native American".

SCARIEST SENATOR

The endless night of the Gillibrand mind has produced yet another euphemism for killing a human* baby. Tired "reproductive rights" is now "reproductive care". "Care", of course, means crushing baby's skull after it is old enough to cry. This Senator is a very scary broad.

Q: Where does a woman's right to off her own baby come from?

A: I asked you first.

*Try this with a baby animal and you <u>will</u> go to jail.

Gillibrand Glossary

Red cap: see "lib-ral bait"

LIBERAL LOGIC: ILLEGAL alien invaders now outnumber the million American babes aborted every year.

HUH

The least feminine women are the most likely to be feminists. Huh. Those who demand tolerance for gays are the least tolerant of straights. Huh. Gender choice killed sex equality the first time a guy competed as a chick. Huh.

Buttigieg is running for President <u>and</u> First Lady. Who can compete with **that**? Huh.

Coming soon: <u>Basic Anatomy For Lib-rals</u>. (Pete can buy one for his husband)

Huh.

AND YOU THOUGHT OUR MEDIA/THOUGHT POLICE WERE OUT OF TOUCH...

After a single introduction, our liberal-compliant "news" media have <u>hidden</u> Pete Buttigieg's husband. Even <u>they</u> know America ain't havin' this. How would you introduce them? "Ladies and Gentlemen, may I present Mrs. Pete Buttigieg, President of the United States, and his/hers/its husband, Mr. Whats His Name.

Note: Not to look for logic amid insanity, but shouldn't the twinkie be the "wife"?

QUIZ

Q: Who got put up quicker than Henry's wives?

A: Pete's husband.

THE STALIN SMILE

Q: Why so hard on Mrs. Buttigieg? He (she/whatever) seems so...so <u>nice</u>.

A: This socialist in sheep's clothing will have you envying Venezuelans before 'Casio-Cortez can kill the cows. Huh.

FASHION SENSE

If you are afraid to wear a (plain) red cap, you know what America will be like should Cory, Kammy, Bernie, Petey, Gillie, or Pochahontas be elected.

RE THE ABOVE...

Q: Why don't lib-rals wear red just to see how their side operates?

A: They already know their comrades pull down statues, smash store windows, and stab police horses in the face. But, hey, they <u>recycle</u>. Cumbaya, pig.

DON'T CRY FOR U.S., VENEZUELA

Usta race with a Venezuelan. Taught me how to stuff a front tire into a rear so you could carry-on a new set o' slicks to Caracas. Last I heard he could still wear a red cap without getting punched inna face. Onliest thing for a lib-ral to love 'bout Venezuela is that socialism has turned the richest country in South America into a wealth-shared third world hellhole. Fucking cumbaya.

FULL CIRCLE

Recent revelations reflect badly on Democrats. The liberalestablishment "news" media have begun referring to Chelsea Manning as a "him". Huh.

ASK PETE'S HUSBAND: "We should not use religion as a cudgel. But God hates Trump." –Mrs. Pete Buttigieg. Huh.

YOUR OWN TV SHOW

You "recycled" old-growth lumber from a barn just as real farmers have been doing for centuries. You made a huge profit. Now you want a cookie. Consider: I picked up a watering can (Remember them?) and disturbed a tiny spider who had called it "home". She rappelled away from the intruder and, thinking the lout had left, ascended the lifeline, ate her web for later use (she did <u>not</u> call it "recycling"; she works for a living), and moved to a better neighborhood. Atheists beware: this shit is going on all around you. Dumbass.

Progressives note: she did not ask for gov-mint help. Dumbass.

TORTURE A TURTLE, STRANGLE A SKUNK

A yard spray is "manufactured for" Farnham Pet Products which is somehow related to Central Garden & Pet Company which is labeled Adams Yard Spray (Whew!). Screw it onto a garden hose and it sprays just fine. Coverage capacity is a secret but, hey, the bottle has a clear sighting strip so you can monitor how much product is left...uh, no you can't. The sighting strip is on the front of the container (You think I am making this up, don't you?), proving that no Adams/Central/Farnham employee has ever used this stuff. **Note:** Aw, don't sell them packaging engineers short. If packaging engineers can configure 6-pack rings so suited to strangling sea turtles, and Yoplait yogurt cutesy backwards containers/death traps for baby skunks, squirrels, raccoon, opossums, etc., why, packaging engineers can Find A Way to stand in front of a pesticide nozzle.

Dishonorable mention: PAKTECH-OPL.COM produces rings to hold juice, peroxide, and rubbing alcohol bottles in pairs. These little horrors are hard plastic, replete with teeth to engage the bottle neck. They're a bitch to remove. When they grab a small animal's neck they add cutting and bleeding to the strangling creature's misery. If Adams/Farnham/Central bottles are stupid, PAKTECH-OPL.COM pairing rings are insane. Welch's juice and Member's Mark toiletries use them. Welch's and Walmart are usually responsive to consumer complaints; please join me in this. What Walmart does, the union dues dummies will follow.

Note: Feminists finally figured out that Yoplait yogurt cutesy backwards containers/small animal death traps were designed for <u>them</u>, which is why they canceled the next Million Mom March For Late-Term/Partial-Birth Infanticide and will instead protest Yoplait yogurt cutesy backwards container/ small animal suffocation devices...just kidding. But the next time some broad says, "Awww..." when shown footage of still more baby mammals slowly dying in Yoplait yogurt cutesy backwards container/small animal slow suffocation-strangulation devices, check out her refrigerator. Then tell her to shut the fuck up.

P(m)S: The Yoplait yogurt cutesy backwards container/small animal slow suffocation-strangulation device has a punt (with a "p"). Translation: deceptive packaging. "Empowered" women buy it anyway. Hear me roar.

Onna plus side: The Olympic Committee now has a way to sex athletes. If it buys Yoplait yogurt cutesy backwards container/small animal slow suffocation-strangulation devices, it's a g...g...g...girl. It if buys Yoplait yogurt cutesy backwards container/small animal slow suffocation-strangulation devices and wants to punch you in the face, it's a b...b...b...bloated girl. Do-dah.

FLEA BUS

Warning: Spray your shoes, sox, and pants legs before visiting the dog walk, the Dollar Store, or <u>any</u> elementary school.

AGEIST, RACIST, SEXIST <u>OLD WHITE MEN</u>...OOPS!

A mostly-white young woman would deny them freedom of choice, rip them from their parents, and take them home for <u>her</u> pleasure, without a care that they would not survive the climate change. She would shift a Sitka spruce to Sudan; a yucca to Yukon. Inside the funhouse of her unwittingly racist mind, importing European plants (and people) is racist; bringing chilies and cabrons from Caracas is A-OK.

Q: Is brown racism better than white racism.

A: To any Democrat, why, yes. Yes it is.

Tucker Carlson aired AOCs detritus; neither noted how perilously close she was to knowing something: the millennium-old concept of crop rotation as practiced by any Medieval serf-farmer, who also left 1 in 3 fields fallow every year (field rotation) and planted hedgerows to control wind & water soil erosion while providing bug-eating birds a crib. Pshaw! Today, serfs who no speaka spray shit that shines in the dark onto the soil that springs your 'sparagus while clad in haz-mat suits & respirators. Don't need no birds when you chemically kill every living thing in sight. It's called "soil fumigation". Bon appetit.

Note: Picturesque hedgerows have no place in modern "farming". 100 acre fields better suit planting & harvesting with huge combines. This insanity drives down the price of produce <u>and</u> creates dustbowls, as it did in the 1930s when it caused a worldwide depression in the process. When the water today's "farmers" are stealing from our aquifer (down 30' in many places) runs out, history will repeat itself. Meanwhile, yuppies yearn for yucca in Yonkers. Yay.

Anthem: <u>Brown Bad Deal</u>

He smiled as we parted, 'cause he didn't know,

That we lost our Yucca, at the first fall of snow.

-Equatorial African Kwanza Karol

Ps: But they...they stewards o' thee lay-ind!

Bullshit. Land stewardship died the day agribusiness learnt how to grow bumper crops on soil that was worn out from irresponsible farming methods by dumping chemical fertilizers onnit. They then get $enator ubidy to send over A irrigation pee-vit, dree-il they-seff A way-ell, an' they is good ta sling water all over the place: <u>some</u> of it raych-es the roots, doncha know. Nutritional value? We gits pied by thee ton, son, not fer no sissy nutrients.*

*Consider spinach, thought to be iron-rich. <u>Read the label</u>. Spinach does a great job of absorbing iron from the soil; it cannot produce it. Grow it in the same dirt year after year, way-ell, they ain't no arn fer eet ta 'sorb. See: crop/field rotation, 1,000 years ago. Dumbass.

CAPITALISM CURES CORTEZ

Channeling 'Casio, a Canarisie Chassid is offering state-specific seed packets. Already available: Alabama (collards & Okra), Border States (Coca & Marijuana), Massachusetts (Saffron & Rainbows), Reservation (Tobacco & Peyote), and Texas (Barbecue, Barbecue, & Barbecue).

1,000...HELL, 5,000 years ago, farmers Found A Way to get precious water to the roots rather than have half of it blow away on a sunny, windy day. I guess they had soaker hoses. Who knew?

PURE CAPITALISM: GOOD; GOV-MINT-ASSISTED DEPRADATION: NOT SO MUCH

Exit I-75 at Hamilton County, ~~Florida~~ Northflorida: a moonscape awaits.

Q: Fire? Flood? Earthquake? Tornado?

A: Mine.

Q: Why not tell The Mine to leave a swath o' trees along US 129 to hide the devastation and keep down the toxic dust?

A: T...T...tay-el The Mine to do sumpin?

Q: OK, why not <u>ask</u> The Mine to leave a swath o' trees along US 129 to hide the devastation and keep down the toxic dust?

A: A...a...ast The Mine to do sumpin?

Seeing a Hamilton County Commissioner so shaken, I moved on up and called the ~~Florida~~ Northflorida Department of Environmental Protection. Tee-hee. The unelected career bureaucrat thought I was from The Mine. "We glad yaw called. We comin' out termorry to inspec y'alls scrubber stack #7. Y'all might could put thee feel-ters back innit teal we done gone. That'll be stack #7. Baa."

Dang. I hauled off and called environmentally-concerned Representative Elizabeth Porter, who was environmentally-concerned enough to have 'nother unelected career bureaucrat from the ~~Florida~~ Northflorida Feesh & Waaldlaff Commision call me. He was not defensive; he was hostile. "Wut yew wanna know 'bout The Mine?", he asts. "Way-ell", says me, trying to sound as if I was not born & raised down the street from Damnyankee Stadium, "Swift Creek runs fast, clear, and dead. Not a fish...feesh, minner, tay-ed pole, frog, tuttle, 'nothin'. Ah heard it runs through The Mine." "Son", says he, "The Mine don't got nothin' to do with it, and they don't be no 3-ay-ed feesh comin' outta there. Baa."

SEE SOMETHING, SAY SOMETHING

Think reporting a shoplifter is not your concern? Think again. Everything we buy costs more than it should to allow for "shrinkage", industry jargon for loss due to damage, spoilage, and <u>mainly</u> theft. Even Democrats should care: there is no way to pass the cost to someone else.

SANCTUARY CITY BANS PLASTIC STRAWS

Live in a tent, shit on the sidewalk, shoot up in public, but don't you dare drive in the carpool lane, unless, of course, you recycle. Cumbaya.

CONSISTANCY IS NOT A LIBERAL TRAIT

Coupla very sick kids died shortly after their dumbass Sanctity of Motherhoods snuck them into the U.S. and the left went nuts. A million babies are aborted every year, many after they are old enough to cry, and lib-rals call it a "women's health issue". See? Offing your baby makes you healthier. Who knew?

DUMBASS

Mrs. Smolett's enabling a monster aside, the world now knows bitch can't spell.

WAAA! (WISHING AMERICA APOLOGETIC AGAIN)

You traded your Obama Food Stamps for a Trump Chevy Impala. Feelin' pretty sporty...<u>not so fast,</u> Home. "But...but...(lib-rals love to say, 'but...but...'), some are richer than others!" Yeah, and some will get laid and some will ask to borrow your dildo. What's your point? Dumbass.

NEEDY HEROES*

As more TV ads show women taking charge and mitigating danger while their man-buns splutz in doe-eyed admiration, more women work two jobs to pay for the parasite who lives with them. How has feminism been working out for YOU?

*Fi said "heroines", you'd think I'm talkin' smack. Thank a teacher.

GALA GUEST EDITORIAL

Forward: Vagrants spread syringes and scat on sanctuary city sidewalks. We are culturally insensitive. Guess who lib-rals viciously attack?

"You kill unwanted children, kow tow to a Deep State, and put political rivals in solitary confinement via a mutt named Muerrer, but it took you 3 generations of bad parenting/bad teaching /bad "news" media to get there. #&%+$@¢#! [Pshaw!] Your lib-rals still allow vestiges of the valor of your Revolutionary War and the genius of your Constitution; **we** erased the Tienanmen Square Massacre* in 30 years. Now: <u>Where Horrywood</u>?"

-Ho Lee Fuk, Department of Re-Education

Peoples Democratic Socialist Republic Dictatorship of China

*Chinese correge student: "What country did that happen in?" (actual quote)

American college "student": "We're outta beer. Get Gramma's bong."

Att progressives who identify with the female gender: sit down and shut up. In China, you would have been killed at birth for being the wrong sex. Be thankful that lib-rals will never do that here...Oops!

MISSION STATEMENT: "Designed by 8 year-olds for 8 year-olds."*

The chocolate coating on the mini-donuts melts at room temperature (75°F).

(You think I am making this up, don't you?)

Q: Why doesn't anyone at Little Debbie know this?

A: They buy Tastykake.

Note: Refrigeration results in a bag-shaped brown brick.

*When they 14 and pregnant they switch to mayonnaise sandwiches.

GILLIBRAND GLOSSARY: intolerant: opposes taxpayer-funded infanticide a/k/a late-term & partial-birth abortion.

MORE MARLIN VS MULLET

Mrs. Thomas: "My son is a Supreme Court Justice."

Mrs. Smollet: "My son tried to start a race war."

Reminds me: Scorned skank Anita Hill was immediately offered a professorship. This is sooo unfair. Angela Davis had to murder a judge to get hers.

BEST SHOT

All saints are former sinners. Satan is <u>gonna</u> get to you; the best you can do is to make her work for it.

PAY YOUR OWN DAMN DUES

On their first try, family-owned Bush's offered B.R.E. (Beans Ready to Eat.) What a concept. No more doctoring with brown sugar, spices, etc. to make them edible. Knowing they couldn't touch the taste, Stokeleys whined, "But...but...ours cost more to make". Hard to imagine.

Q: Will you buy crap just to pay someone else's union dues?

A: I am not a Democrat so, no. NO, I won't.

WHATEVER

"...whatever it is you choose to believe in..." –Mrs. Pete Buttigieg

See? See? You will still be allowed to believe in traditional marriage; you will just not be permitted to <u>say</u> it. And you thought the left was intolerant.

Q: Will I be allowed to wear a red cap while hunting?

A: H-h-hunting? With <u>what</u>?

SKOOL OF HISTORY, HORTICULTURE, ECONOMICS & GEOGRAPHY. Maxine Waters, Principal

Q: Why would you trade our booming economy for the socialism of South America?

A.O.C.: I wouldn't. I've always opposed the Confederacy. I want a system like Botswana. They wear the coolest clothes, and yucca plants will grow there. We'll <u>teach</u> them to recycle.

PELOSI PARTY PLATFORM
Our guy won: "The people have spoken."
Their guy won: "Investigate, impede, impeach."
Q: What else does your Party have to offer?
A: Huh?

RE THE ABOVE: PER GOV. Gavin Newsome, Californians who can't afford health insurance will pay for illegal aliens' health care. So Dems **do** have somethin'

DO NOT LET THE NAME FOOL YOU. Elizabeth Fleming Warren may not be a tribe member, but she is .01% Slapaho.

IT COULD NEVER HAPPEN HERE
Isis bans books, destroys historical structures, attacks those who dare to differ, enforces dress codes (no red caps)...Oops! I musta meant lib-rals.

> **Note:** This is sooo...unfair. To our knowledge, no lib-ral has ever thrown a traditional marriage couple off a building. Yet.

> Q: So, are right to life folks safe?

> A: So, for now?

> Q: So, when did the word "liberal" come to mean the opposite*?

> A: So, I asked you first?

*the opposite: see, "closed minded"**

** closed minded: see, "intolerant"***

intolerant: see, "liberal"*

****liberal: see, <u>cannot speak</u> absent a "so" and a "?".

BALLS IS BALLS

Electric cars do not have to be wimpy. The QE2 reaches steamship speeds courtesy of the world's largest electric motor, albeit with juice supplied by a buncha God-fearing diesel-powered generators. <u>Balls</u>. Closer to home, **listen** to a diesel-electric locomotive accelerating under full load. <u>Pure balls</u>.

Q: When does a <u>Ford</u> pull a train?

A: In high school.

SEXISM ALERT
SEXISM ALERT
SEXISM ALERT
######

HEAR ME ROAR

The 10-inch gopher tortoise could snap a finger off; the 20-inch gopher snake could barely break the skin. Guess which one put bitch into hysterics.

THE BOYS DO IT, SO THE GIRLS WILL DO IT. MINDLESSLY.

Q: They celebrate, sure, but why do the boys tamp it down a bit when they are demolishing a tiny country in, say, a soccer match by, say, 11-0?

A: Because the boys are encumbered with a sense of sportsmanship, some decency of deportment, and a hint of compassion.

EQUAL PAY FOR EQUAL...WHAT?

THE GIRL IN RAPPELLING class required no courage as she was not afraid. Even when two of us had to drag her dangling derriere over the parapet, she looked at us with that idiotic, "Oh well, the boys are doing it; it must be safe" smile. Oblivious to the danger, she actually giggled. Now, the guys had guts because they knew, they fucking **knew**, that their carabiner may have been forged on a Friday afternoon or, worse, on a Monday morning by a bloated butch who was feeling icky. **Next:** Receptionist Runs Off Customers Every Twenty-Five Days But Males Are Toxic. (Liberals: <u>You</u> assumed that "receptionist" meant "chick".)

AND I THOUGHT **MY** REINCARNATION/PURGATORY SUCKED: Bones is a person trapped in a dog's body <u>and she knows it</u>.

LORD, SEND ME A SIGN...

You know your racing days are over when you start making mistakes with the tractor. **Note:** A high-strung racebike can kill you; a low-strung Farm-all will <u>kill</u> you.

Q: Would campaigning a less fractious bike make up for slower reflexes?

A: Absolutely, just as soon as gravity and inertia increase their reaction time.

Q: Wouldn't a horse be safer for both endeavors?

A: The horse has more brains* than you, and even the tractor, but he has no kill switch, so it's a wash.

*If he is a mule, he has <u>lots</u> more.

############################
GALA HERETIC
SECTION############################

P ROLIFERATION

Every organized religion has screwed the pooch except maybe the Quakers.

Q: What do you tell progressives who call the Ten Commandments "suggestions"?

A: "Buy a dictionary."

ABOMINATION

I know lotsa chicks, and so do you, who can fathom kissing a girl but want throw up at the <u>thought</u> of two men sucking face. Don't tell me there is no difference.

PREACHING TO PRICKS

"Good works are filthy rags." What Pastor tells nasty folks who tithe well.

"Faith alone is a clanging gong/tinkling cymbal." Now you're onto something, Parson, but it'll cost you some playing customers who want to go home and not help a living soul.

Jesus was the original first responder; His <u>actions</u> showed us how to live. If you need it spelled out, read The Sermon on the Mount. You'll see lotsa stuff 'bout helping your neighbor; not some prattle about knowing Jay-is-us.

REPARATIONS

I know, Trump is divisive, but Democrats keep picking at the slavery scab. The Party of victimhood, welfare-ism, racism, and class warfare would cease to exist in a unified country where most folks work for a living. Dumbass.

Ps: Democrat machine politics have controlled Detroit, Baltimore, Chicago, Newark, etc. for decades. How's <u>that</u> been working out for Black folk?

HEY MOE! LET'S DISARM OUR SHIPS! YEAH, THAT'S IT!

A 1,000' tanker is boarded by a 20' motorized rowboat because company policy prohibits guns. Duh. Were the skipper to ship granddad's shotgun, this shit would cease. With a load of blue whistlers in his felonious future, even the silliest Somali would keep his distance. Duh. (Dems: am I going too fast for you?)

DEMOCRAT DUPLICITY: "Kamala's too white. We need a young **black** woman to defeat ageist, racist, sexist Trump."

BACHELOR TIP 3: PHOTOGRAPH your new sweetie. Cameras can't be blinded by love.

TARIFF GOOD

For the Fourth, Scripto Aim'nFlame Special Edition Grill Lighters (Calico Brands, Ontario,CA) features an American Bald Eagle and an American Flag on the handle. They are, of course, made in China.

PELOSI PATRIOT

How much do you have to hate your Country to support the import of every undocumented unvetted unvaccinated indigent illegal alien invader that every third-world hellhole spews? Ask Nancy.

Q: Can she disguise her treachery by calling Trump a hater?

A: Half the voters have been indoctrinated by NEA (union, no competency testing) teachers and aging hippie lib-ral professors so, why, yes. Yes, she can.

Q: Is Hillary a hypocrite for accusing Trump of collusion?

A: Clinton is a communist so, why, da. Da, she is.

Note: Choose your candidates on the basis of age, sex, and race, then call Trump an ageist sexist racist. See: <u>Rules For Radicals</u>, Chapter I.

Q: By Hillary's hero, Saul Alinsky?

A: Da.

SHE: 'WE'RE PREGNANT". HE: WHAT'S THIS 'WE' SHIT?".

Condom. I.U.D. Monthly pill. Night-before pill. Morning-after pill. Still, she Finds A Way to get knocked up, then waits until baby is old enough to cry before killing him/her. Bitch <u>needs</u> old white men to govern her uterus.

LIBERAL VISION FOR AMERICA

Dad-less homes. Free school lunch <u>and</u> breakfast lets Mom sleep in. Yuppie "food anxiety" program gets this extended all summer (Will Ms. Sanctity of Motherhood **ever** get out of bed?). This is not the black family tradition. This is not the white family tradition. This is the lib-ral wet dream. This is fucked up.

The blacks' new overseers, the Democrat Party, presided over the breakdown of the family unit (see: Lyndon Baines Johnson) to create a new class of do-nothing/know nothings. Who else would vote for a Pelosi, a Schiff, or a mayor named Pete who says he has a husband?

Note: Replace "black" with "product of 3 generations of bad parenting and aging hippie lib-ral teachers", and you'll know why the black, white & brown family unit has been usurped by minimum-wage day care strangers and NEA (union, no competency testing) teachers. "It Takes A Village", you say? How's <u>that</u> been working out for America. Dumbass.

####################
GALA HOMOPHOBIA SECTION
####################

ANTIFA(SCIST): see: "IRONY"

Test a "progressive". Tell him/her/it that you are conservative; say this while being black. You may not be lynched, but you sure as hell will be doxxed. Now you know what life will be like if the Democrats win in 2020. Do-dah.

Note: Exaggeration? Only if you haven't heard A.O.C., Liz P. Warren, Kammy Harris, Cory Booker and/or his wife, Pete Buttigieg (Or is it t'other way 'round? It's hard to remember who is the bride; they're both somewhat butch.) lately.

Q: What do "progressives" call the above?

A: Homophobia.

Q: What do **you** call a male "wife"?

A: Insanity.

Q: What would Booker T. Washington say to Cory Booker?

Q: Before or after he bitch-slapped him?

Q: What do Booker T. and Cory have in common?

A: Both have had their stories suppressed by liberal-compliant "news" media.

Q: Do you believe in "live and let live"?

A: Yes, like most Americans. It's the queers who won't shut up about it.

Q: Would "progressives" dox Booker T.?

A: Da.

DEMOCRAT CANDIDATES, 2020.: "They move so smooth, but have no answers." -Cat Stevens, <u>Where Do The Children Play</u>

DADDY! DADDY! WHAT'S A TITTY BAR? (Smart answer: "Uh, how would I know?")

GPS tells the boss where his rigs are, so truckers suddenly obey speed limits. No more makin' up time so they can stare at a stripper. Families do not miss the **Girls! Total Nudity!** signs, and drivers now spend spare time at the chrome shops. **Note:** Airplane pilots and race car drivers flat black everything in their line of sight.

Q: Why do truckers blind you (and themselves) with bling?

A: Because they're stupid.

Q: They drive all day for a living. Why not cut down on glare rather then produce it?

A: 'Cause they're stupid.

Q: Why do they seem to **enjoy** the world's most boring job?

A: They're stupid.

Q: Why Jake brake into town ("saves brakes & clutches, doncha know") 'steada taking their foot outta it and (quietly) coasting, which is (almost) free?*

A: Haven't you been paying attention? They're stupid.

*Owner-operators ghost into and out of town because their name is on the door and <u>they pay for the fuel</u>. They are not stupid.

TRANS FATTY: SEE PORTLY CROSSDRESSER

Feed the dog or cat tofu and you <u>will</u> get bitten. Godfearing animals keep their proper diet; sinful, no-sense man now wants to choose his/her/its gender. Why, next thing you know, women will choose to kill their babies. **Prediction:** they'll call it something unrelated like "health issues" or "reproductive rights"*, right up to <u>and after</u> the moment of birth, then kvetch when invaders bearing anchor babies are stopped at the border. When one is unfettered by logic or shame, life is simple. Can I get a Cumbaya?

*Here's a reproductive right: **stop breeding**, Stupid.

PSYCH 101: THE DR. O.J. FORD DEFENSE

On scene: "Oshifer. I don't know how I got here and I don't know how I'll get home, but I absolutely, positively had one beer."

In court: "They...they laughed at me. I'm stupid."

Witness Warren: "Any woman accusing a man must be believed."

Deplorable: "In all things I believe them, except for maybe two- Everything they say, and everything they do."

-I do not remember writing this, but I absolutely, positively had one beer.

THE KKK SOMETIMES...YIKES! LET'S PULL DOWN ALL THE CROSSES BEFORE COLIN SEES 'EM!

New Nike Logo: Company President hand-jobs hate hustling has-been quarterback.

(Betsy Ross would have slapped both their faces.)

I DIDN'T EVEN VOTE DEMOCRAT (ACTUAL GROCERY STORE EXCHANGE)

Q: You have a sleeve, a grill, and a pound o' piercings. Why do working people pay for your food stamps?

A: Because they're stupid.

WHAT, THEY GONNA CUT MY HEAD OFF? A Stupidity Section must at least <u>mention</u> Islam.

HONEY NUT CHEERIOS wants me to "scan a buzzcoin". Silly me. I was gonna go out in the yard and play.

JUST DO IT: SOMEONE should read Colin the rest of the Fredrick Douglas letter.

July 4, 2019:
DEMOCRATS CELEBRATE
THEIR INDPENDENCE
FROM REASON

Warning: may contain inconvenient facts that lib-rals will dismiss as homophobia, sexism, misogyny, ageism, etc. while declaring Kammy Harris too white, Joe Biden too old, Cory Booker too closeted, and Trump too successful.

F LAY-IG DIE (FLAG DAY)
Usta hang my Betsy Ross to piss off the ~~Florida~~ Northflorida rednecks (it just **looks** kinda damnyankkee*). Now I fly it to annoy them lib-rals that kiss Kaepernick's butt and to remind me of what Massachusetts was like before it became gay.

*See? South America (Mississippi, Alabamy, Northflorida, etc.) has NEA (union, no competency testing) teachers, too, cepin' they call theysells "taychars". Y'all.

THE USEFUL IDIOTS OF KARL MARX

"Accuse others of **your** treachery." -Communist Manifesto

Communist: re-write history, foment class struggle. See also: Democrats

Conservative: Betsy Ross would slap Colin's face; Crispus Attucks would <u>hurt</u> him.

<u>Again</u> (pay attention), our Country's founders did not decide to get themselves some slaves. They were born into a system which had existed since Biblical times; still does in Islam's idiotic world. They set up a system of government

which put an end to that abomination in 2 generations, an eyeblink in human history. When the showdown came, a lotta white boys died to Get It Done.

Note: Many black soldiers died fighting for freedom during the Civil War*, yet their numbers pale in comparison to the white soldiers who died fighting <u>for someone else's</u> freedom. Put another way, the "reparations" have been paid in blood. Are you still waiting for Colin to simply say, "Thank you"? # Me Too.

> *Civil War: ask your NEA (union, no competency testing) teacher
> to look this up.

WAAA!*

When Obama was elected, ¾ of Republicans remained "very proud" of their Country.

When Trump was elected, ¾ of Democrats did not. Spoiled brats/whiney bastards.

*Wish America Apologetic Again.

STRANGERS TO REASON: THE WHINEY WAIFS AT WAYFAIR FURNITURE COMPANY

Lib-ral logic: Children sleep on shelter floors. Stop making mattresses. Cumbaya.

Deplorable logistics: Fire the strikers. Hire the Mexicans. Do-dah.

When the Mexicans pull themselves up by their own bootstraps, as they often do, <u>they</u> can re-hire our whiney lefty millennials as housekeepers, lawn men, pool boys, etc. No college degree will be wasted, as their liberalmarxistprofessors have taught them nothing useful. (Hating your own Country is not useful.)

AGAIN, North <u>and</u> South, the slavery issue has been settled in blood. May we move on? We live in the finest Country on Earth (Thank you, Jesus): let us work together to make it even better.

ACTUAL COOKING DIRECTIONS 'Place in 400° oven for 45 minutes. Caution: product will be hot." Thank a teacher.

LOOK, JANE, LOOK! SEE KAMMY STAMMER.

Uh...yes...I own a g-g-gun. Buzz. For p-pr-pro...for safety. Zaapp. But the Second Amendment mmpffschmor, and semi-automatic zdkah-buh pltopza. The NRA is felopzid. If elected, I will executive order devpotec. Now, no more questions!

~~FLORIDA~~ NORTHFLORIDA FOLLIES

The President of (name withheld) advised voting for Putnam "counta De-Santis don't be one of us". High praise, indeed.

FIRST YUPPIE WINE, NOW YUPPIE WHISKEY

"This small-batch single-malt is matured in two different woods to give it exceptional flavor and complexity." Shoulda stopped there, but they didn't. "Toffee and vanilla give way to toasted almonds, honey, and floral aromas (swear to God) with a long, decadent finish enhanced by oak and dark chocolate." Bullshit. It tastes like whiskey. Ps: If I wanted a candy bar, I'd have <u>bought</u> one.

MORE BULLSHIT

Top-dollar Tide claims "fresh scent", which is too true if you think eau de wet dog is "fresh". You can fix this by adding a splash of disinfectant, but you shouldn't have to. Hot Tip: store brand is half the price and twice as good. Free-market capitalism will see Tide improve or go away, unless some unelected big-gov-mint aficionado (see: Democrat) fucks it up.

PROGRESSIVE

Why do dress shirts still come with spare buttons? Post-feminism, there's not a broad around can sew one on. Onna plus side, after three generations of ex-hippie parents, there's nary a first grader can't stoke gramma's hash pipe.

IF SNAKES COULD SCREAM...

She's anti-hunting and runs over snakes.* supports no-kill shelters** and human infanticide right up to the moment of birth. She is caring. She is a monster.

*Snakes suffer <u>silently</u>, you see.

**Q: Who expends limited resources on moribund animals, thereby lessening the chances of healthy (for now), adoptable ones?

A: Sunshine, Sky, Peyote, and other dreamers who buy dog food with peas, carrots, and watercress on the label. Cumbaya.

HER HERO

Q: Why does she support that parasite?

A: He watches her grandbaby while she and her daughter go to work.

How has feminism been working out for YOU?

PROGRESSIVE PLATFORM: We are not proud of our Country (even for the first time), but vote for us anyway.

GALA DEMOCRAT VISION FOR AMERICA SECTION

"You white people wanna close the border to prevent the browning of America."

-Democrat candidate for Presidente de los Estados Undios (del Norte).

Not so fast, cabron. Life is swell. The lib-ral vision has you sit the porch. Smoke the blunt. Sport the tattoo/body bling that your food money paid for (the dumbass taxpayers bought your ABT groceries). Kids? Daycare. Meals for Mother's mistakes? School lunch. And breakfast. And now that some sniveler has invented "food anxiety", free meals go on all summer, so every sanctity of motherhood can sleep in or keep partying. This is not the Black family tradition. This is not the White family tradition. This is fucked up.

The Black's new overseers, the Democrats ("They'll vote as we <u>tell</u> them to.") engineered this "Great Society" mess to create a new class of know-nothing/do nothings. Who else would vote for a Pelosi, a Schumer, a Schiff, or the male bride of a twinkie? Dad-less homes, free meals extended all summer, and bitch sleeps in 'till Oprah comes on. Yay.

Note: Now go back and strike the word "black". America is becoming a land of sorry sumbitches of every ethnicity. When 51% of the population gets on the dole, **it's over**. They'll <u>have</u> to vote Democrat "to keep our shit coming". Next time some dreamer mentions "income redistribution", hand him/her/it a copy of George Orwell's <u>Animal Farm</u>. Do-dah.

THE DECLINE OF A NATION CAN BE SEEN IN HOW MUCH BULLSHIT IT ACCEPTS

Russian Putinista: Our President is a badass KGB-trained killer.

American Progressive: <u>Our</u> President is the bride of a twinkie and cries a lot.

The fact that this asshole has been taken as a serious candidate for Commander-in-Chief scares the crap outta me. If that is "homophobia", count me in. Bitch.

HOW TO SURVIVE IN A SANCTUARY**

To the lib-ral mayors who say they will not tolerate Antifa violence against conservatives but tolerate Antifa violence against conservatives: If you arrest anyone who wears a mask, most of those cowards will stay home.

To conservatives who are attacked by Antifa: If you rip their masks off, most of those cowards will run away. "Waa! He took my mask! All I did was hit him with a bike lock. Waa!*

*"Waa!" Not to be confused with "W.A.A.A.!" (Wish America Apologetic Again)

**If you do not see the irony, you are a lib-ral.

MORE PICKIN' ON PETE

He is liberal, Democrat, and his "husband" is less masculine than he.*

Q: With all that going for him, what liberal could fail to be enraptured.

A: One who lives in his City.

*Look for logic elsewhere.

Note: Beto writes babytalk, eats dirt, and plays with shit, and coupla lib-rals don't like <u>him</u>, either. Go figure.*

*Easy one. Beto once had his wife w-w-<u>watch the kids</u>!

YOU KNOW YOU VOTED CORRECTLY when Hollywood imbeciles stage a reading of mutt Mueller's report.

POT RACK (SEE? THIS THING WRITES ITSELF)
Yuppie Broad: Eeeuu! Those pots must get dusty up there.

Married <u>Once</u>: Right. Let's put 'em in a cabinet where something with lotsa legs can crawl around in them.

Hot Tip: If you find black rice in a pan that's had plenty o' privacy lately, it's not black rice. Eeeuu.

BONES

MY AGING COW DOG REGAINED much of her conceit when, AMA, I resumed feeding (supplemental) table scraps.
Q: What does steak bone, fat, and gristle have that packaged food lacks?
A: The will to live.
Note: If you feed your carnivore from a bag that has peas & carrots on the label, this is over your head.

TEA PARTY
Boston was once the hotbed of anti-establishment thought and action; it was the center of freedom from big gov-mint tyranny.
Q: What do you call what Boston is today?
A: Ironic.

ALL THE NEWS THAT FITS
Iran's attacks on oil tankers in the Strait of Hormuz did not affect our gas prices...Oh, that's right. We are now energy independent.

Q: Are you still waiting for Wolf to mention it?
A: # Me Too.
(In the United States of Apology, there would have been gas lines. Do-dah.)

FAREWELL TO FLATS
Q: Why aren't tires made from insulin vial rubber?
A: So, because it's red? (Practicing my yuppiespeak)

IF THE SHIT FITS
The toddler throws a diaper and craps the floor. The cat seems grateful when you clean it up; the dog, disappointed. Seems that rolling in it was the <u>nicest</u> thing he had planned. See? Dogs **are** more fun.

THANK A LOBBYIST: TRAIN cars carry 10x more than trucks at a fraction of the cost.
Q: Why'd we get a <u>highway</u> network?
A: Because Standard Oil and Firestone Tire & Rubber wanted it that way. Try and surmise why it was. U get 3 surmises (And you thought <u>Who Framed Roger Rabbit</u> was a kids movie.)*
*Rockefeller & Firestone bought the trolleys and pushed them off a cliff. Access to Los Angeles is now a breeze.

HE LOWERED MY TAXES. THEY SMASHED MY STORE WIN-DOWS.
2 ½ years and still no tyranny from Trump. Lotsa tyranny from Antifa, though.* If you <u>like</u> mob rule, vote "progressive". Dumbass.
*Aw. Three (3) Dems have disavowed Antifa.

DOGS 'N' DEMS

Cat: Eeeuu! That "mozzarella stick" is a turd rolled in kitty litter.

Dog: Sprinkles!

Q: What's the dog's name?

A: Beto.

Q: I thought it was a female.

A: That's the other one,

Q: What's her name?

A: Pete.

Q: Uh, how can you tell them apart?

A: One eats dirt and plays with shit.

CATHOLICISM MADE EASY

Grabbing up an anchor baby as you jump the border can be tough. Now there's a nicer way. Show up in AOC's District with a yucca plant. If she's busy hectoring Border Agents, gift it to any Archbishopric. In the name of the Father, and of the Son, and of the Dumbass Taxpayers, Amen.

Q: So, when will His Excellency harbor illegalalieninvaders in **his** neighborhood?

A: So, when the Pope shits in the woods?

A STRONG INCENTIVE TO DO NOTHING

Q: If Republican is the Party of Lincoln, and Democrat is the Party of George Wallace, Lester Maddox, and James Earl Ray, how did the Republicans allow the Democrats to garner the black vote?

A: Stupidity.

Q: With their history of knocking down black people with fire hoses and axe handles, how'd them Dems Get It Done?

A: Handouts.

Q: How do they pay for those handouts?

A: They don't. You do. Dumbass.

Q: If you can get all you need while sittin' on your ass, why work?

A: Ask someone else. I quit.

BUT **I'M** THE RACIST

While Democrats fret that Kammy isn't black enough (no racism <u>there</u>), the Trump economy eliminates the fodder that race baiters/victimization hustlers Jackson, Sharpton, Pelosi, Waters, and their media organ, CNN, <u>need</u> to promote their otherwise empty agenda. Successful blacks frighten them; conservative blacks scare the bejesus outta them.

Q: WHO DECIDED TO PLACE wall outlets at the baseboards?

A: Somebody young.

GALA SHE ONLY HAD ONE BEER, #METOO PAGE
##########

CONGRESS SHOULD PASS A LAW TO ABOLISH CONGRESS
As a meanspirited republicanuntiltheybecamehaplessandgutless, I am generally opposed to yet more rules, but I would support legislation requiring manufacturers to **use** their products. That way, Little Debbie's Dad would know that her chocolate donut icing melts at room temperature, Rockport Shoe Company would discover that suction cup soles track in suction cupfuls of dirt, and the housewife-engineers who make homeowner-grade pressure washers would learn that heavy equipment wants to be drawn, not pushed like a grocery cart, on lawns, gravel driveways, and other uneven terrain. (Pulling instead of pushing also keeps the hoses from getting underfoot. Duh.) For guidance, behold any locomotive, which pulls rather than pushes its charges whenever possible. **Note:** a Ford once pulled a train, but that was 36 years ago.

Q: Is this the same Ford that fears flying but commutes to Hawaii?

A: The same. (and you thought Little Debbie was a sticky mess)

Q: How?

A: Tor Highertail set up the Con-Tiki Skank Shuttle many moons ago.

Q: Is the Con-Tiki Skank Shuttle still running?

A: Where've you been? The S.S. Con-Tiki has been replaced by H.H. Hirono, which ferries illegal aliens who make it to the Aloha State to N.H.J.* with O.P.M**

Gillibrand Glossary H.H.: Haole Hoekboot

*Not Her Jurisdiction

**Other People's Money

P.S.: Upon arrival, Dr. Ford stated that she did not know where she was, had no idea how she got there, had only one beer, and asked to borrow a pair of land legs. "She is a woman; she must be believed", said a woman who once claimed to be more than .01% Slapaho. Look it up.

Note: The cumbaya crowd is encouraged to contribute to fordfraud.org, administered by P. Fleming-Warren, with a .01% of the proceeds promised to starving Slapahos who are forced to fornicate at the Hilo Hyatt-Regency Hotel. Aloha.

BASED ON BULLSHIT

Harris hawks housing help based on skin color; calls Trump a racist.
Pelosi posits that "citizen" means "white"; calls Trump a racist.
Gillibrand gushes that women don't lie; calls Trump a sexist.
Honorable mention

1- My name is Pete, I have a husband, and I'm running for President/ First Lady.

2- Well, I'm not actually a member of a <u>tribe</u>... -Pocahontas

3- Cory can't compete: he has no husband. -Curly

4- Hon, check out this "avocado". -Beto

BUT...BUT THEY'RE DISHWASHER SAFE!

To save herself the drudgery of p-p-peeling an egg (the horror!), she buys egg-shaped Tupperware (swear to God) that must be washed. Hear me roar.
Note: Careful, guys. Lose a lid and you forfeit a testicle.

HER SAFE SPACE: Sen. Hirono encourages unvetted, unvaccinated, undocumented illegal alien invaders to **mainland** U.S.A.

TESTOSTERONE LEVELS THE COMPETITION

She advocates for women but celebrates her maleness with man-suits and **man**-ner-isms. The 100th ranked male tennis player will beat the top female every time, but I had wondered how the 100th best male would fare among female soccer players. One Womens World Cup later, it turns out he did quite well. Re the aggressiveness of a man **plus** the self-absorption of a woman*: Has anyone thought to <u>test</u> this person?

Q: For drugs?

A: For dick.

*Deny away; her/his victory antics speak volumes about MEgan

P.S.: **Teach Your Robots Well.** "We will speak with anyone who agrees with us." Thank you, MEgan, for summing up the "liberal" approach to life, and for reminding us that an athlete/political commentator is no more absurd than a singer or an actor* feigning competence in that arena.

* Actor: pretends to be someone else for a living (hardly a noble profession), yet an entire generation of dumbed-down Americans (thank any NEA, union, no competency testing teacher) actually **listen** to these assholes.

TE-RAY-ZA'S HUSBAND

Trump pulls us out of the boneheaded Biden/Obama/Kerry-Iran treaty.

Q: How long before Iran starts screwing with our "allies" who stayed in?

A: Right...about...<u>now</u>.

"HOW DOES IT FEEL?" -Bob Dylan

Nancy Pelosi just had the race card played on HER. Cool.

~~PATRIOTISM~~ PREJUDICE ON PARADE

Q: Had the Womens' (more or less) Soccer Team been conservative, would New York City's mayor/clown have given them a ticker tape parade?

A: Had the Womens' (more or less) Soccer Team been conservative, they would not have dragged our Flag across the field like a rag, dropped it on the ground like a piece of trash, nor sullenly sat during our National Anthem*, so, no. No, he wouldn't have.

*Aw, did CNN forget to air <u>that</u>, too?

DAMMIT, JANET: <u>PRIORITIES</u>

YOU can end San Francisco's sanctuary city status <u>today</u>. Document a dog stepping in (human) feces* an/or getting stuck with a used drug needle. PETA will jump their shit.

*Justice is served.

LIB-RAL LOOKING GLASS

Nancy must be excused her conceit that all "citizens" are white. They don't be no black folk 'roun de Pelosi Palace, nohow.

NOT TO SAY THAT THE CNN crew gushed over MEgan, but the grips were seen spreading sawdust on the floor.

GALA TITLE NINE SECTION
##########

CHAPTER 1: HILLARY'S HOYDENS AD OBNOXIA

Axiom: Your parents are the products of ex-hippies. They know nothing, so you know nothing. Stay that way and do as you are told by your lib-ral overseers. <u>No diversity</u> (of thought) <u>allowed</u>.

Rule 1: Drop all the feminine graces, pronto. Instantly adopt every boorish male mannerism to the extreme, unencumbered by any sense of shame, remorse, regret, compassion, or common sense.

Rule 2: Rule 1 prepared you: mindlessly mimic <u>what</u> the boys are doing absent a clue as to <u>why</u>. Thus unfettered, you may over-celebrate every goal, however meaningless, as when you are up 11-0 over tiny Thailand. Remain incapable of differentiating between a hard-fought win and a hollow victory. This "empowers" you to force yourself into an occupation that does not suit you by playing the sexism card, and then really sucking at it. You can do anything you want. Teacher said so.

Rule 3: Disrespect the Country that provided the perks to put you where you are. **Note:** Younger (and better) people than you have fought and died (<u>their</u> opponents were shooting at them) to defend your right to drag your Country's flag on the ground, so be an ass and Just Do It.

Rule 4: Gracelessly use your sports status to proport political prowess, just like any singer or pretender (actor). In this you will be abetted by fawning liberal-compliant media as long as you hate Trump. (For an account of actual air time afforded conservative jocks*, singers, and pretenders [actors], see page 1,000.)

*Q: Is it OK to refer to Womens' (more or less) Soccer Stars as "jocks"?

A: Since I suspect that some of them have something to stuff into one why, yes. Yes, I believe it is.

Absolutely, positively unrelated to the above and I had one beer (the Dr. O.J.Ford defense): I watched the pussy paw a ball around the room using only her feet. Well, OK, she (rarely) used her head. Suddenly I know why a Womens' (more or less) Soccer game is called a "match". Meeow...uh, I mean, Hear Me Roar.

######################
TITLE TEN (SURPRISE!)
######################

CHAPTER 1: "DAD"? WHAT'S "DAD"? A SINGLE MOM DOES JUST FINE.

After working all week, Mom is mowing, painting, and changing the oil. Daughter is playing sports. Son is playing video games. (Permissiveness follows Mom's guilt over having them raised by strangers in "daycare".)

Son becomes a waitress. Daughter joins the Army and meets her first love. Their (same sex) "marriage" fails when she Finds A Way to get knocked-up. She goes to work while her new hero stays home to watch the baby. The deadbeat's spawn is now a relative of yours. Grandmother. (Congratulations)

Q: So, how has feminism been working out for YOU?

A: So, it Takes A Village?

P.S.: Did I mention that the son is now a waitress?

HOW'S MY ~~DRIVING~~ WRITING? CALL 1-800- (you know the rest...)

EIGHT (8) TYPES OF BIRTH PREVENTION, AND BITCH GETS KNOCKED-UP. Knocked-up. Hyphen? Sure, but no hymen.

YOU CAN'T FIX ~~STUPID~~ CRAZY

Our Founders feared that farce of mob rule called "democracy"; they set up a republic.

Democracy: One person, one vote. Lunacy. (Look around you.)

Republic: Wanna vote? Be an asset, not a parasite. Contribute fuck-ing <u>something</u> to society. Dirtbag demands a say? Move to Somalia. They'll think you are a genius.

Socialism: Gov-mint sanctioned mob rule by force. Relax; you get free college so you'll be an educated welfare recipient (Yay), 'counta they don't be no jobs. Lotsa mind, speech, and gun control. Dead-beats love it: they get free shit, they minds is already shot, they speech is like this, and they guns was tooken away by the po-lice years ago.*

P.S.: Socialism and it's more ballsy twin, communism, have killed more people and bankrupted more countries than any system of government known to ~~man~~ person, yet the Left wants to Try It Again here.

Q: Are they that stupid?
A: They are that insane.
*The Left will always allow them to say things like:
"Gramma! Borry me your hash pipe! We got 2 weeks to vote."

FINE CUS-WEEN

Q: What does it mean when the chef comes out and "drizzles" something on your food?
A: About ten bucks.
P.S.: Q: Can you make rice/tapioca pudding? A: Yep.

Q: Is it nearly as good as Kozy Shack? A: Nope.

DOUCHEBAG

He fawned over finally getting on a CNN talk show and promptly proceeded to reveal that he hasn't a clue how the world works. Hard to imagine I once thought David Crosby was cool. Please tell me they didn't really save his fat ass with a liver that was earmarked for a child.

GRAND FUNK ~~RAILROAD~~ OMEGA-3 FISH FAT

They put it in a squeeze bottle and included a long-handled measuring scoop. Still, it maddeningly migrates and you **will** get some on your hand. Three (3) washings later, your hand will still smell like...(do the math). I have caught, gutted and eaten almost every species of fish in North American waters, fresh and salt. Some were mild, some not, but nothing prepared me for the infernal funk found in a feline food supplement. Not to say it <u>stanks</u>, but when you throw out the Welactin-treated esculent* that the dumpster-diving stray cat refuses, seagulls <u>will</u> circle your house. In Utah.

NOTE: One (1) call to Nutramax Labs got them re-thinking their formula**.

Hard to hate a firm that:

1- Instantly responds to crabby customer feedback.
2- Prints "Proverbs 12:10" on the box.
3- Employs a customer service rep as nice as Jessica D.
*When we learn a new word, we USE it.
**Obviously stolen from (the other) Mr. Crab.

HILLARY'S DREAM COME TRUE: Cut defense spending but hire "soldiers" who draw full pay while knocked-up.

###########################
GALA YUPPIE SECTION
###########################

BACHELOR TIP TWO: PEELING GARLIC (SO, "KNIFE" MEANS CHEF'S KNIFE?)

First, gift (yuppie for "give") the Cuisinart to the nearest* yuppie (he'll offer $2 for a $200 machine and ask for a payment schedule: just <u>give</u> it to him). A knife has handled anything that needs to be done to food for 10,000 years. Lay the flat of the knife on the clove and whap it down. With the other hand, missy. Partly crushed, the skin'll come right off. Do-dah.

*NY: the co-op next door

SF: the refrigerator box next to your tent**

RI: across the table

MA: the mirror

**We jest. Successful San Francisco yuppies live in their Beemers. Ask your mom for a down-payment and you, too, can vacate the cellar.

FUN FACTS

Q: So, why won't lib-rals* debate conservatives?
A: So, they can only bring emotion to a fact fest?
Q: So, is that like the yuppie bringing a knife to a gunfight?
A: So, it was a whistle?

*"yuppie" and "lib-ral" are, of course, interchangeable.

SO, IS IT TOO LATE FOR AMERICA?

SO, I ASKED YOU FIRST?

So, not to say that 3 generations of aging hippie bad parenting and lib-ral NEA (union, no competency testing) teachers have dumbed-down the populace, but Alexandria Ocasio-Cortez, Ilhan Omar, Ayanna Pressley, and Rashida Tlaib all <u>got elected</u>? So, this is some scary shit?

IT'S OVER THEIR HEADS

So, after enduring the Clintons and the Bushs, the American people finally got what they need? So, a rough-hewn, no bullshit Davy Crockett businessman who is not part of the entrenched bureaucracy? So, problem: 3 generations of bad parenting, union teachers, and liberal-compliant "news" media have dumbed-down the populace? So, enough to vote resistance to the resistance?

Q: So, what do lib-rals call those who dare display diversity of thought?

A: Racist.

P.S.: Q: So, will THIS be suppressed?

A: xxxxxxxxxxxxxxxxxxxxxxxxxxxx

SO, BLUE BONNET BULLSHIT? So, margarine is NOT ear wax? So, margarine IS floor wax? So, thank God it's not butter?

GALA JUST A TAD POLITICALLY INCORRECT FUCKING SUE ME SECTION

TO MOTORCYCLES AND MAIDENS AND THE MEN WHO RIDE THEM

His name was Lucho. We wondered (but never asked) why a Chinaman had such a Spanish-sounding name. Master Mechanic at The Great Escape Motorcycle Shop, which catered to road racers (the type of racing, not the street need-for-speed imbeciles), he'd tune your Duke and then test-ride it, alighting as if on air despite his diminutive size. Once aboard, he'd pick his way through traffic with the ease of a cowhand on a cutting horse. Had you ever raced, you could sense the cool competence. (The floorboards & fringe crowd may stop here.)

Clinging to common Caucasoid confusion over where Chinese ends and Japanese begins, I often showed up with sushi for lunch, nevermind that Lucho steadily seemed to stow something Spanish in his lunch pail. Turns out, the guy was from Ecuador, the son of Chinese immigrants to that charming Country. He spoke Mandarin Chinese (we think) and elegant, almost-Castillian Spanish; English: not so much. One day the owner groused that while Mr. Lucho was a wizard with a wrench and a dynamometer, he was a bit off-putting to customers who wanted an explanation of their bill (Did I mention that motorcycle racers tend to be tightwads?). "We got this, Boss, pipes up coupla us, vowing to teach the bantam Bolivian some American.

Somebody surmised that it would be easier to learn limericks, so we began with a selection from the American Man of Letters du jour, Andrew Dice Clay. (Problem?) Our choice for Lesson One was the classic, Little Bo Peep, to wit:

"Little Bo Peep, fucked her sheep; blew her horse, licked his feet...etc."

Little Luncho diligently drilled on this Masterpiece of the Spoken Word for days. Sensing, real wrongly, that he was ready, we called the Boss into the back and stood our star student on the dyno. Having already been promised that we'd get him laid, the torque-curve's transcendental tuner proudly put forth:

"Riddle Bo Pip, frucked her ship; brew her whore, ricked his fit..."

The critic's cliché about there not being a dry eye in the audience instantly came true, except that there were a few wet pants as well. Needless to say, we called him "Rucho" from then on.

Note: Coupla years later, who shows up for an endurance race but the little Uruguayan. Due to his profession we had never seen him quite clean, but there he was in pristine leathers aboard an impeccable racebike. (Racers will practice on any damn thing, but they bring their best on raceday and proceed to risk the entire edifice [and their own ass as well] for a second a lap.) I was reminded of how easily that small Salvadoran shot through traffic on a test ride... Well, no wonder! The kid was <u>fast</u>!

Lookin for a moral? Get nothin, 'cept maybe y'all might not be too quick to stereotype folks. ("Liberals" may disregard: this shit's over your head.)

P.S.: Yes, we said "Ecuador", "Bolivia", etc. Coulda proffered Paraguay or Peru, for all <u>you'd</u> know. Thank your lib-ral NEA (union, no competency testing) teacher.

Final thought: Il Lucho quickly grasped the intricacies of our illogical language.

Q: If Jimmy Kimmel mocked Melania's accent, and she speaks five fucking languages, would he not make fun of Lucho, who "only" commands three?

A: Who cares? I stopped watching Kimmel when he playfully pointed a shotgun at the camera(man). I'm a "gun nut"; he's the "I didn't know it was loaded" fool.

"YOU DID NOT DELIVER ON THE TITLE OF YOUR THESIS: **D**."
Well, Professor, YOU try finding a maiden in a motorcycle shop.

NOW, GET THE WHIP...

The dog shakes rainwater off at the door. Don't care 'bout no mudroom getting wet, but her poor ears whap-whapping on the doorpost makes me cringe.

Q: Why doesn't the cat do this?

A: Shit. The cat expects you to <u>dry</u> her.

Note: The pussy likes you to wash <u>and</u> dry her. (Time well spent, by the way.)

INCONVENIENT FACTS, "INSENSITIVE" STATISTICS

Q: Can (the minority daughter of legal immigrants) be stripped of her Miss Michigan title for stating unflattering (to the left) facts and/or "insensitive" (but too true) crime rate statistics?

A: Bro. Miss Michigan can be stripped of her title for wearing a MAGA hat. And she was. Thank any "liberal".

Note: As long as we're being insensitive, it is a fact <u>and</u> a statistic (and you thought that "filler" 2-credit course was useless) that lib-rals rate dead last in charitable giving, far behind conservatives & Independents. Do-dah.

Q: But...but <u>why</u>?

A: By definition, donations were traditionally not made with O.P.M.* ('Course, the Clinton Foundation changed all that.) *Other People's $.

MORE CUS-WEEN

Outta condiment for ye squimps? (~~North Florida~~ Northflorida for shrimp) If'n you have ketchup and horseradish, you have cocktail sauce.

Note: If you have ketchup and horseradish <u>sauce</u>, you don't.

BETTER FARMING THROUGH CHEMISTRY ("STEWARDS OF THE LAND", MY ASS)

"...make sure he farms well, lest the pastures become waterlogged, the soil exhausted..." -Ken Follet, <u>The Pillars of the Earth</u>

The perpetrators of modern farming could learn much from medieval monks. When his ruined soil (Why crop rotate when you can chemically fertilize?) from huge fields (Remember hedgerows?) blows into the next county (Remember the dustbowl?), your local agribusinessman will suddenly call hisself a "farmer" and stick his hand out for yet 'nother gov-mint subsidy (onliest thing keepin' stuff sproutin' is buncha pee-vits playn-tid at taxpayer offense...I mean...expense).

Hedgerow: Usta control wind/water erosion and provide habitat for bug-eating birds. Now hinders huge combines; the birds all be day-id (soil fumigation).

Fumigation: Clad inna haz-mat suit and respirator, someone who snuck here injects death into the dirt. Onna plus side: them green beans glow inna dark. Bon appetit.

WHAT'S "PASTURES" AND "PROVERBS 12-10"? Cows is raised in feed-lots, standin' in they own shit. They <u>need</u> antibiotics.

########################GALA
PUSSY/CAT
SECTION####################

N AIVETE'
Owner: "Sit, Stay! Roll Over! Pull this cart! Fetch! Catch! Retrieve!
Dog: "Whatever you say Boss."
Valet: "Get off that (couch, trophy shelf, keypad, Ferrari, etc.)"
Cat: "You talkin' to **Me**? Seriously? In <u>that</u> tone? Watch me not move. Ass-hole."

Yep, cats are a bit set in their ways. Call 'em c-c-conservative. I like that in a person. I love my bitch, too, but she reminds me of today's NEA (union, no competency testing)-educated, I mean, <u>taught</u> "liberal" know-nothings who so willingly serve as the "useful idiots" of Marx and Engels. Thank a teacher.*

*And/or ex-hippie parents. (Pass the bong, Gramma)

AMERICANS ABHOR ARROGANCE
Wishing our Women's (more or less) Soccer Team would get their butts kicked seemed vaguely unpatriotic until I watched them drag my Country's flag on the ground. At least MEgan didn't sulk while sitting out the National Anthem...Oops!

Lib-ral: But...but (lib-rals love "but...but...") they have a right to do that.

Sentient: They have a right to spew racial epithets; doesn't mean they should. Dumbass. **Note:** "dumbass" is a non-racial epithet; <u>anybody</u> can be one.

GENERAL NEUTRAL

Yikes! The sexes <u>are</u> different (lib-ral: "Seriously?"), and I can prove it. Tupperware causes women to shriek, "You lost a lid!" and "<u>That's not Tupperware; throw it out!</u>" Men, of course, think that any cheap plastic tub that retains water (sorry) indefinitely is Tupperware. Silly us.

Note: A time capsule (Remember <u>them</u>?) from 1957 was recently unearthed. It contained a set of then-cutting edge Tupperware. There was water under the rim. Oh, and a lid was missing.) Ladies: 1-2-3-Shriek!)

P.S.: Gentlemen: YOU tell her that you lost the lid when you used it for fishing worms....

STUPIDITY EQUALS STOMACH SURGERY

The pinch-faced (Is there any other kind?) yuppie broad told the vet, "We always put the rubber bands away, but the cat can still get to them". Swear to God. Her wife nodded in solemn agreement. The Good News: none of them will breed. Yay.

Note: The cat is straight, but she's been fixed.

"NO BARRIERS, NO BORDERS; WE ALL JUST NEED TO COEXIST" intoned geopolitical expert Katy Perry from her gated, guarded community.

Lib-rals: change woman to "identifies as female"; conservative to "deplorable".

"PHOTO I.D.S ARE RACIST!", says Maxine Waters. To attend her events, you need...wait for it...a photo I.D.

POLITICALLY CORRECT SECTION ########### (just kidding)

RAISED IN DAYCARE, THEY WANT THE GOVERNMENT TO BE THEIR MOMMY

Their lives were harsh, their government did them few favors, yet they astounded the invading Nazis with how hard they fought to defend Mother Russia.

Their lives are easy, their government "assists"* them far too much, yet they astound the world by how much they want to allow invaders into America.

* **"assist":** pay for their food so they can buy tattoos and piercings. Yay.

SAVE YOUR BUSINESS: <u>STAY HOME</u>

Q: Does "equal pay" include an adjustment for time lost during maternity leave?

A: Shit. They should subtract stipends six days out of each and every month.

Bumper Sticker:

Save the ~~whales~~ water coolers/copy machines/co-workers/customers: <u>stay home.</u>

COMMUNES & CATHEDRALS

Medieval monks were usually self-sufficient (more from Ken Follett and Mr. Franklin Bauer, the high school teacher who spoiled me for most college professors). They built their own living quarters, barn and stables; they dug fish ponds, raised livestock and grew crops. Unlike hippie communes, sloth was not tolerated.

They followed St. Paul's rule (Bible-quoters may check this) of "No workee, no eatee", which is Latin (well, Aramaic, actually) for "Go be a deadbeat somewhere else". **Note:** Today's dirtbag simply finds a Democrat with a handful of O.P.M.* He/she/it** will salivate to spend stupid out of his sluggishness*** with someone else's simoleons. Thank any lib-ral.

Gillibrand Glossary

*Other People's Money.

** We're LGBT-WTF friendly 'round here.

***Don't nothin' get a grifter goin' faster than fantasies of free shit.

THE DON LEMON DEFENSE

Idiot: Your Honor, I blew by the school at 90mph, but the prosecutor is a racist.

Judge: How do you know <u>that</u>?

Idiot: CNN told me so.

Judge: Case dismissed!

Q: Can a white guy play the race card?

A: Only if he is a lib-ral.

Q: Does Don Lemon call <u>everybody</u> a racist?

A: Heavens, no! Don Lemon only calls you a racist if you dare to disagree.

Q: With him?

A: Heavens no! Don Lemon calls you a racist if you disagree with <u>any</u> black person.

THE CITY SUCKS, TOO. I thought The Beatles burped up the worst lyrics known to music until I remembered Chicago.

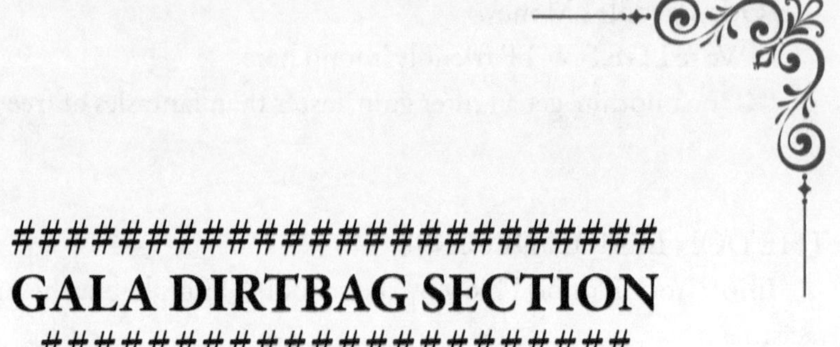

###########################
GALA DIRTBAG SECTION
###########################

I HATE DEBT REDUCTION COMPANIES
Every time some deadbeat gets his debt reduced and/or "forgiven", prices go up to cover it. As usual, folks who pay their bills carry the dirtbags who don't.

DEMS <u>TALK</u> SENTENCING REFORM; TRUMP <u>DID</u> IT.
Today's aware blacks are far less likely to be hustled by Sharpton, Jackson, and other race baiters/victimization hustlers. They know Trump is no racist. Why do the Democrat operatives at CNN persist in calling Trump, and everyone else who dares to disagree, racist? Easy one: <u>they</u> are racist, through and through. <u>Everything</u> they report is seen through a racial prism. Cop defends himself, shoots back. Is the cop black? Is the criminal, I mean, "victim"? is Kammy black enough? Is Cory androgynous enough? Will Beto stop playing with shit long enough to support reparations?

Q: Why <u>do</u> the Democrat operatives at CNN assign "racism" to diversity of opinion?

A: Because they know, they fucking <u>know</u>, that come election day, buncha lib-ral know-nothings, fully indoctrinated by lib-ral teachers, ex-hippie parents, and fake "news" media, will emerge from mommy's basement and vote as they are told; maybe mask up and smash coupla capitalist store windows onna way home. Who else would expect, or even <u>want</u>, student loan "forgiveness" anda buncha other gov-mint free shit at the expense of their freedom? Freedom is an empty promise to those who cringe in cellars. Until an unvaccinated illegal alien invader drops in and takes his stash and video game, this societal carbuncle will support taxpayer-funded giveaways for all.

ACCUSE THE OPPOSITION OF **YOUR** CRAP. -Hillary's Hero, Saul Alinsky

Conservatives are slow learners. During the Apology Years, it was made clear that to disagree with a "person of color" on <u>anything</u> makes you a racist. Michelle and MSNBC told me so. Now, Omar supports boycotting Israel, AOC would jail our Border Agents, Tlaib likes Al Qaida, Pressley hates America, the entire Democrat schtick is identity politics, but Trump is "dividing the country along racial lines". Gimme a break.

Note: Trump is handling the harridans all wrong. They are strong. They are invincible. They are women. On the other hand, they want to be patted on the head and told, "Yes! I agree with everything you say!" Hear me roar.

P.S.: Policies pushed by the left have already turned the richest South American country into another third-world hellhole. Other socialist experiments are circling the bowl.

Q: Why do Democrats want to try it here? Are they insane or just stupid?

A: Yes.

Q: Why does my kid think South America is "like, Alabama and stuff"?

A: Ask his/her/its NEA (union, no competency testing) teacher.

Q: Can you be stripped of your beauty queen title for citing inconvenient (to the lib-ral establishment) facts and "insensitive" statistics?

A: And for wearing a MAGA hat.

'Nother Note: If Trump wins a second term, this shit will stop. Scares the crap outta all them closemindedestablishmentliberals.

DEMOCRAT THEN: SORRY for "all lives matter". NOW: Sorry for deporting aliens. SOON: Sorry for America...Ooops! <u>Done</u>.

GALA EXCOMMUNICATION SECTION

"What we hay-ive heah...is a failure...to excommunicate." -Cool Hand St. Luke

"I'M TAKIN' SOME TIME WITH MY QUIET FRIENDS..." -Van Morrison

"SUNDAY MORNIN', COMIN' UP." -Philberto Phantomini

The Sunday morning air is crisp. Dog is out in God's Own sunshine, chewin' a bone. Kitty-Kat's sniffin' at my fresh cuppa coffee. Nice to see that all is right in their world. Me, I'm not real hung over, and ham & eggs is callin'. Why would I want to fuck this up by going to church? Proverbs 12:10.

HOLISTIC HOMOPHOBIA HEALING HUG-IN

"Hi. My name is Pete, I have a husband, and I'm running for President." He should have stopped right there. If an entire generation voted for Barack rather than think themselves racist, they sure won't want to feel homophobic.

Note: Ilhan can beat Trump by declaring herself a lesbian. No safe space can shelter a sexist, racist, Islamo-homophobe. The yuppie vote is HERS.

ACCUSE THE ENEMY OF BEING **YOU**. -Hillary's Hero, Saul Alinsky

"His home was burglarized. That's too bad." (Per CNN, "too bad" is now "snarky".)

Q: Who would accuse Trump of being snarky?

A: Someone snarky. (see: accuse the enemy of being YOU)

Note: Ain't lib-rals amazing? They can tell what you are <u>thinking</u>! Well, think <u>this</u>: with socialism, college is free, but they don't be no jobs. Why, you'll be the smartest burger flipper they ever wuz. Ast enny Venezuelian.

Q: Clear it up: wassa difference between socialism and communism?

A: Both take all your stuff. Then, one sings Cumbaya; t'other kills you.

INNER CITY BLUES <u>Where Do The Children Play?</u> – Cat Stevens

The Rules: Trump says Baltimore is a mess. Don Lemon says "mess" means black; therefore, <u>Trump</u> is a racist. Got it?

Phil Berto: Pesky fact: 80% of black children are born out of wedlock.

Pocahontas: So, slap 'em in daycare! What's the problem?

Phil Berto: Wouldn't it be better to rebuild the family ethic?

Pocahontas: Why? Daycare child warehousing allowed me to get where I am.

Phil Berto: Chief, that's exactly my point. (The interview inexplicably ended.)

KARMA KATCHES KAMMY

In the second debate, Harris' hypocrisy haunted her. It couldn't have happened to a nicer person. When questioning overworked, understaffed (thanks to Congress) Border Patrol agents, the Kamster was imperious. Now she was reminded that she packed a pistol while smoking weed, then imprisoned 1,500 souls for doing the same. Worse, she committed the abomination of withholding exculpatory evidence. Filthy stuff; nasty person.

OMAR SCARED TO RUN GAY. It's OK, Ilhan, **it's OK.** We don't throw queers off buildings here. That's YOUR job.

################
LEGENDARY LIBERAL
TOLERANCE SECTION
###############

E DUCATION vs INDOCTRINATION
Test Teacher's tolerance: tell him/her/it that you are conservative. Say this while being black. Do-dah.

WHAT TO DO...

Problem: A thoughtless person gifted (yuppie for "gave") you a Chic-fil-a gift card. You really, really want the free lunch, but your friends might see you enter that tabernacle of intolerance.*

Solution: Borrow a buddy's Antifa mask. On the way back to Mom's basement, you can toss a brick through the bookstore window (they have c-c-conservative books in the back; I've <u>seen</u> them), maybe kick over a capitalist newspaper dispenser or two.

*The owners believe in traditional marriage, but they (get <u>this</u>) will hire those who disagree. W.T.F.!

WORLD STAGE

A white supremacist once flew a Betsy Ross flag. CNN was all over it.

A World Cup champion dragged Old Glory on the ground. CNN: not a peep.

Note: At least she didn't throw it in the dirt like a rag...Oops!

Liberal Allowable: Aw, she was just caught up in the moment.

Deplorable Retortable: So was I when I pinched your wife's ass.

LIFE AFTER DEATH DEMS

Q: After she takes your coal, your car, and your cow, what else could 'Casio covet?

A: Your soul.

Q: Can I keep my Betsy Ross flag?

A: If Trump is re-elected, why, yes. Yes, you can.

DEBATE

<u>Not one</u> Democrat operative/"moderator" asked Pete. "If you are elected, do we call you Mrs. President, Ms. President, Madame President, or fucking First Lady?

Note: Pete's husband would be "First Gentleman". Do-dah.

P.S.: This skunk knows that Trump did not include Neo-Nazis, and so do you.

P.S.: You think I'm making this shit up, don't you?

THEY USTA BE BADASSES (READ THEIR BOOK)

Q: With so many anti-semites in the Party, why do Jews still vote Democrat?

A: All those years as God's Chosen People hebetated* their survival skills.

Q: When did they stop being The Chosen People?

A: When Jesus fired the Pharisees.

Q: Why don't you call Jews "Jewish People"?

A: I'm not running for office.

Q: Who else calls Jews "Jews"?

A: Jews.

*Learned a new word today. So did you.

WOMEN'S SOCCER TEAM RULES: No Betsy Ross flags! You must drag the Star Spangled Banner in the dirt.

SCARY: MASS SHOOTING casualties are approaching what Democrat-controlled Chicago suffers every weekend.

AND YOU THOUGHT "HAPLESS" AND "GUTLESS" COVERED IT...

All those establishment never-Trump Republicans who tried to keep Davy Crockett out of their private club now have their hands out for re-election funds. PATHETIC.

Senators, Congressmen, you didn't heed the call-
You stood in the doorway, you blocked up the hall-
The people spoke; all you did was stall.
The times they are a-changin'. -Bob Berto

HOW QUEER!

I usta get castigated (Ouch!) for calling queers "queers". Now, lotsa queers call themselves "queers". Anything's better'n "gay", of course, but it kinda takes the edginess out of it, which is probably the point, O.K., try this:

Q: If straights are called "straight", couldn't queers be "bent"?
A: Over.

ACCUSE THE OPPOSITION OF BEING **YOU.** -Hillary's Hero, Saul Alinsky

Bob DeNero wants to punch him in the face. Johnny Depp could shoot him. Kathy Griffin holds up his severed head facsimile. Madonna would bomb the White House. A NYC play shows a dozen men stabbing him to death. Oh, and Trump's rhetoric incites violence.

The left is correct: our system is unjust. For threatening to blow up the President and all those near him, Madonna should have skipped the slammer and scraped up shit in San Francisco. Bitch wasn't even arrested.

P.S.: Any obedient establishment lib-ral will deny that dad-less homes, children raised in daycare, mindlessly violent movies & video games, and the dissolution of the family have anything to do with the proliferation of psychopathy.

AS AMERICAN AS APPLE PIE & RABBIT PAPRIKASH (HUH?)

Dad arrived in New York City with the shirt on his back and a capacity for insanely hard work. Gov-mint "assistance" (hand-outs) had not yet been conjured. He learned a trade (well, two, actually) and taught himself damn good English. Ably assisted by a steadfast wife (Huh?) who managed the home (Huh?), husbanded the house (Huh?), and took a job _after_ the children were reared (Say, _what_?), they put 5 kids through private primary & secondary school and 3 through college by busting their asses. They became as American as any New England so-called blue blood and passed their love of Country on to their family.

Comparison: If you are waiting for some Somali devil (don't you dare call her "Somali-American") to thank the Grandest Nation on Earth for easing her escape from her native hellhole, well, # Me Fucking Too.

P.S.: Dad & Mom came here legally. Lib-rals: have your favorite tenured hoax look up "Ellis Island" for you. You will both be amazed.

I WONDER IF TRUMP WILL be able to deport as many (800,000) "wonderful people" as former President Obama?

GALA RACE BAITING/ VICTIMIZATION HUSTLING PAGE

Director of Finance: SPLC

New Money Counter: Beyonce'

Timekeeper: Shelia Jackson Lee

Board of Directors

"Rev" Al Sharpton

"Rev" Jesse (Jussie?) Jackson

Cory Brooker

Kammy Harris

Kirsten Gillibrand (not really her name)

Pocahontas Fleming Warren (not really an Indian)

Joaquin Castro

Julian Castro

Fidel Castro*

* Old devils never die- They just look that way.

QUIZ

Q: Mr. Lemon, can you ask a question that isn't racist?

A: You are asking me that because I'm black.

AND YOU THOUGHT **REPUBLICANS** WERE GUTLESS

During the debates I hoped that one (1) Democrat would instruct Don Lemon that it would be OK to ask one (1) question that is not racist.

I WISH THEY'D MAKE UP THEIR MINDS...

Warned not to call nobody "oriental" no more, I kiddingly (and accurately*) called my friend a "Chinaman". With tedious predictability, the left went nuts.

Note: An "oriental" can be from half the planet; an "Asian" from ¾. "Chinaman" narrows it down to a quarter of the globe. See? Three times as accurate, and a lot more fun.

P.S.: Hung Wang (his real name) agrees; pinch-faced white yuppies may fuck off.

BUT...BUT...I PITCH FOR CINCINNATI

Q: So, I can't say "Eye-rakian" no more?

A: Bro. You can't wear that red hat no more.

~~SNEAK SHOEHORN~~ CROWBAR IN SOME SEXISM/QUEER BAITING

The Womens (more or less) Soccer Team spawns sexism <u>and</u> homophobia (but no kids). Returning victorious, they shouted, "Lock up your wives!", at once espousing lesbianism <u>and</u> adultery.

Q: Can the men say that?

A: Shit. The men can't wear red hats.

GUTLESS VS BETSY ROSS: If the KKK hoists a "Just Do It" flag, Nike will have to cancel the entire line. Yay.

ARROGANCE: SHELIA JACKSON Lee is not on white OR black people's time. Shelia Jackson Lee is on Fuck You time.

######################
LIBERAL LARGESSE SECTION
######################

JUSTICE

I believe in re-incarnation. Be a dick, come back as a cockroach. Be especially despicable, return as Maxine Waters.

HELL

You are a waiter/waitress/server working for tips. Your steady customers are Bob DeNero, Maxine Waters, Nancy Pelosi, Barbra Streisand, Joaquin Castro, and Shelia Jackson Lee. #StarveToDeath. **Note:** Aw, Shelia spends <u>your</u> $$$ pretty good.

~~SCHINDLER'S~~ JOAQUIN'S LIST

You...you voted for our opponent? **Doxxed!**

You...you gave him money? **Caravan to your home!**

You...you have a business? **Joaquin Castro's List!**

"I am not calling for a boycott." Bullshit. Why <u>else</u> the list?

"I just want people to think about whom they support." There you have it. <u>Finally</u>, some honesty from the left. Translation: just in case you escaped indoctrination by lib-ral NEA (union, no competency testing) teachers, we get a second chance at mind control. When you think about whom to support, <u>you must think like us.</u>

101

P.S.: Vote for T-T-Trump, be assaulted "in the restaurants, at the grocery store, the gasoline station", etc. -Maxine Waters (You think I am making this up, don't you?)

HOME SCHOOLING

It's on the 'net. Teach Socialism by giving you kid $10 for cleaning the bathroom, then taking $7 back and giving it to the sibling who didn't.

Gillibrand Glossary

Socialism: pays $10, takes back $7, gives it to your do-nothing brother.

Communism: gives $7 to a stranger, takes back your $3, and kills you.

AO-Cortez: gives $7 to a deadbeat, takes your last $3, and kills your cow.

BACHELOR TIP

Changing the AC filter monthly saves lungs and money. Hot Tip: get the old one <u>out the house</u> and into the fire pit (dust mites). Do this, and the pet flea treatment, on or near the 1st so you won't have to keep track. Duh.

ASK DON LEMON

Q: Don, I like vanilla ice cream. Am I a racist?

A: Absolutely not. You are a racist because you dare to disagree with anything any black person has ever said. P.S.: Just don't get a white, blue-eyed dog.

AN ALBINO BUCK HAUNTED the Delaware Valley BDL (Before Don Lemon). No hunter would shoot him. How racist we were!

SEXISM & SPROUTS (SUE ME) SECTION
###################

BACHELOR TIP

You best learn your way around the kitchen, Sonny, 'cause your post-feminist girlfriend (Massachusetts: "partner") thinks she is not allowed.

I usta thought it was quaint when, in her dotage, Mom rinsed food storage bags for re-use. 'Course, Mom lived through the Great Depression, brought on by the dustbowl created by irresponsible farming...Oops!; the worst I hadda deal with was the recent Apology Years. Now, I ain't gonna wash no bag, but I <u>will</u> save one whose only occupant had been a head o' lettuce and use it for bagging cat poop, dog throw-up, things I find in my bathroom, etc.

Yuppie broad (frantic); "But...but...(yuppies <u>all</u> say 'but...but...') if you re-use it, <u>you can't re-cycle it!</u>"

Almost Sentient Being: "There, there. Say, there's a tofu sale at Sky & Saffron's Sprouts, Sprigs, Seeds & Stems Shop. Run along, now."

Note: A Tofu "sale"? Sounds kinda capitalist to me. Hmm. Cumbaya capitalism. Why not? We already have limousine lib-rals and a Barbra Streisand who wants you to hang YOUR laundry on a rope. Why, next we'll have solar energy panel deserts in Vail, windmills in Hyannis Port, an asylum-seeker welcome center in Martha's Vineyard, and citizenship classes in Kennebunkport. Yay.

NO NEWS IS FAKE NEWS

David Duke stated his support for Trump in 2016. CNN told me so. The KKK contributed $20,000 for Hillary in 2016. CNN didn't say shit.

SUBARU SHOWS DAD DRIVING...just kidding

Patriarchy bad; Daycare good.

75% of black, 35% of hispanic, and 25% of white kids live in fatherless homes. How has matriarchy been working out for YOU?

Note: the statistics are conservative; the situation is liberal.

P.S.: 97% of mass shooters are from fatherless homes. They ain't getting' their toxicity from their Dads.

NO PUBLICITY IS BAD PUBLICITY (TELL THAT TO SEAN)

Laura Ingraham: as informative as Hannity minus the kvetching.

SONG FOR XENIA T.

Q: Can anything match crossing the start/finish line at full throttle when the R-6's scream bounces off the race control tower and puts you in a tunnel of howl?

A: Yes.

"If I was blessed with just one wish to take me through my lonely life, I'd wish to go back to the day that I met you." -Lillian Axe

LIZ P. FLEMING WARREN says It Is Good to raise kids in daycares staffed by strangers. Obedient lib-rals comply.

WHY ON EARTH WOULD OUR CAMPAIGN OWN AN AMERICAN FLAG? -Saul Alinsky

At Hillary's first rally, someone noted that <u>not one</u> American flag was present. Aides bustled to borrow a bunch from local businesses. (CNN's camera crew waited.)

Q: Why not just <u>buy</u> them to have for future use?*

A: Prescience.

*These are the folks who stand in line at the post office to buy one (1) stamp.

Note: Rumors abound that in place of flags, the Democrat National Convention will distribute pitchforks and torches (their words). Hey, if you're gonna doxx somebody who dares to disagree, you better have the right equipment. P.S.: Those who think "diversity" means more than skin color have more than doxxing to worry about. If you support someone who dares to disagree and you <u>contribute</u>, you get Caravanned. Try this while owning a business for your livelihood, you get Listed. Joaquin/Julian Castro Listed.

> Q: When your business is bankrupted and you must go on welfare, what will the Democrats say?

A: Welcome to our Party, comrade.

Q: What do they call creating another parasite?

A: Why, they call it "social justice", brother.

Q: What do we have to look forward to if Dems prevail in 2020?

A: All the above. My brother.

Q: Why doesn't this bother today's "liberals"?

A: Because it doesn't affect them if they are obedient.

SHE **WILL** SNOOP*

If you care about the girl, look to your medicine cabinet.

Q: You mean, hide the jock itch spray?

A: And the Preparation H.

*One broad brought her daughter. They were in my bathroom for 20 minutes. 'Time they came out, they wouldn't even shake my hand,

Related Topic: "That's it! **That's** what I want to do for a living." Bro, if you think podiatrists are weird, wait 'till you have to see a proctologist.

CRONY COMMITS CLINTONICIDE

Q: How can a high-profile suspect on suicide watch commit suicide?

A: Shit. Vince Foster blew his brains out and wrapped himself in a rug.

Clintonista: The dirt I have on you I will take to the grave.

Bill & Hill: Why, yes. Yes, we believe you will.

tps: CNN: The log shows you took 26 flights with Jeffrey Epstein.

B&H: We think it was four.

CNN: Four it is.

CNN TOLD US ALL ABOUT the El Paso shooter; the Dayton devil: not so much. White supremacists get covered; Antifa thugs do not. CNN declined to divulge that both were environmental extremists, as was the Unabomber...What, they didn't tell you <u>that</u>, either?

ATT IL PAPA FRANCISCO: 'Humility" is not the same as humiliating and making a spectacle of yourself.

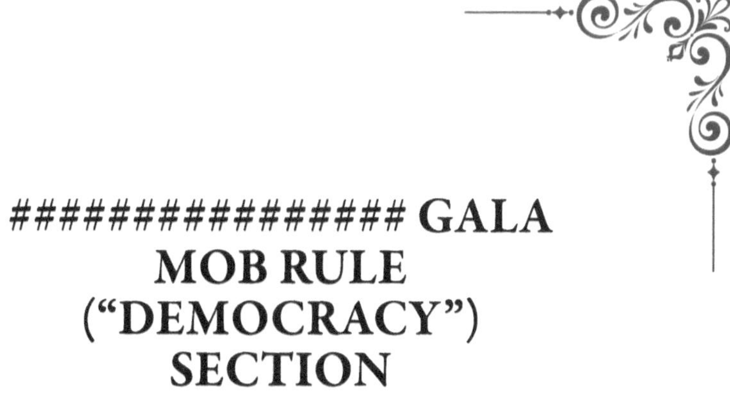

GALA MOB RULE ("DEMOCRACY") SECTION

H E SHOULD HAVE LOOKED AROUND FIRST

Q: Whose wet dream was "one man, one vote?"

A: An ancient Greek who didn't get out much.

THE DEBAUCHERY OF DEMOCRACY

The Founders spec'd out a <u>republic</u>. They presciently feared today's "liberal" mob rule (doxing, caravans, listing, etc.) that are aided and abetted by fawning "liberal"-compliant "news" media. Plus (get this), they expected voters to contribute <u>something</u> to society, not be parasites on it. The nerve!

Those old dead white men were such pricks! They expected voters to wash up, dress appropriately (Huh?) and present themselves at the time of their choosing during a 12-hour period (Huh?) on a pre-set day (Huh?) that was never a Monday or a Friday (Oh, like people don't party all week), having on their person as much identification (Racist!) as they would take to a bar or library, and cast an <u>informed</u>* (Huh?) ballot.

*Not blind obedience to the Democrat operatives at CNN. Hint: get some channels and find a counterpoise. Truth often lies midships.

DUMB DAMN DEAL

You have two weeks to sober-up enough to vote or, if you can't put down Gramma's hash pipe, you can mail it in. Well, why not mail in citizenship apps from, say, Somalia? You may respond in any language except Hmoob. Even Hillary's fucked-up State Department wouldn't let you respond in Hmoob. There will be only two questions:

    1- Wil U vot Demcrat?
    2- Kin U swam?

TRUMP IS NO MATCH FOR THE LEFT <u>AND HE KNOWS IT</u>

Q: He has no doxing, no caravanning to people's homes at midnight, no Joaquin/Julian Castro List. What does Trump have to compete with THAT?

A: That.

WHAT'S WRONG WITH ME?

Q: Why do you call Trump a racist?

A: Uh...uh...because CNN <u>says</u> he's racist, <u>that's</u> why. What's <u>wrong</u> with you?

DEATH BEFORE DIVULGING

Q: Why be a Trump toady rather than a Clinton crony?

A: Last I heard it's 63 times safer. (That includes a man whose dog ate his head,)

Q: Is a dachshund capable of making a head go away in 8 hours?

A: That depends on what the meaning of the word "is" is.

AULD ARKANSAS LEGEND has it that when the Clintons took tarts on a "tour", some o' them chicks were for Bill. -WH

GALA AMERICA THE BEAUTIFUL GULAG SECTION

A T LEAST BITCH KNOWS WHERE TO FIND <u>THIS</u> ONE "My baby daddy". Not "the father of my child". Not even "my baby's daddy". Nope. "My baby daddy." That's the best brainless (And she breeds!) can do, and "culturally sensitive" NEA (union, no competency testing) teachers <u>are not allowed</u> to correct this shit. My baby daddy. Heck, even limousine lib-ral Joe Biden thinks that ghetto fabulous children are "as smart as white kids" (Trump, of course, is the racist here), <u>and they are</u>; they just ain't <u>taught</u> nothin' no more. Joe & Company remain unaware that lotsa white kids are also semi-literate (Who are the real racists here?). Nevermind facts, the truth (there go Joe again) is that in extirpating patriarchy in favor of matriarchy (when they don't be no baby daddy, they hasta be a strong Mom), the feminists got theysells sidestepped by buncha teen moronic moms and they (feminists) don't even know they have fucked it all up. My baby daddy. Indeed.

Onna plus side, one more generation of professionally dumbed-down (thank any NEA [union, no competency testing] teacher) teen moronic moms and we'll be safe from the depredations of China and Russia.

Q: What will keep out a Sino-Russo invasion force?

A: The State of the Union. Be like takin' over Somalia. Nothin' worth stealin'.

Q: Wouldn't they send their prisoners here?

A: Only the ones who really piss them off.

Q: Will there be torture?

A: Of course there will be torture. Ever day ever body wheel be forced to watch Teen Moron Mom and lissen to her say, "My baby daddy". Ever day.

Q: Wouldn't Teen Moron Mom learn to speak 'time she turned 14?

A: Shee-it. 'Time she turned 14, she be havin' 'nother baby daddy ta keep track of.

Q: Couldn't at lease <u>one</u> o' them baby daddy be her husband?

A: Bro. **I** tell the jokes 'roun here.

TPS Report: When he isn't pointing a shotgun at the camera(man) like any "I didn't know it was loaded" fool, Jimmy Kimmel mocks Melania's accent in her fifth (5th) language. YOU were fucking born here. What 'sackly is your excuse? Ast yo baby daddy. Fucking dumbass.

LAWN SPRAY

Treat for fleas within a day or two of mowing for better p-p-penetration. While you're attit, spray that pile o' clippings that your bagging mower picked up. **Note:** mulching mower aficionados may disregard: you've already spread those fleas & flea eggs (and weed seeds & mold spores) all overt you propitty. **Hot tip:** spray, don't soak. You wanna kill fleas & ants, not salamanders, skinks, spiders, snakes*, and other silent sentinels what keeps the big bugs in check.

P.S.: Lessin' you have a spare Bean pump layin' around, the basic garden hose/ spray bottle works surprisingly well. Wear rubber boots and a respirator.

TPS Report: If you earn 6 figures, you have sand fleas and palmetto bugs. Make less, you have fleas & cockroaches.

*If'n you have kids, pets, or legs, you may shoot <u>poisonous</u> snakes. Only water moccasins attack unprovoked, but if you or yours accidentally step on a rattlesnake, the outcome is the same. Do-dah.

CONTEST: WHICH IS MORE moronic: "It Takes A Village" -or- "My Baby Daddy?" Win a pitchfork & torch from the DNC.

ELIZABETH FLEMING WARREN (MOHAWK? NAVAHO?*) ALMOST WINS THIS ONE

Q: What's creepier, mimes or clowns?

A: Rachel Maddow. (*Slapaho)

SO YOU'VE MUCKED OUT FLICKA'S STALL. NOW TRY AN ARK.

Noah traded his Birkenstocks for Noconas (look it up) on Day One; hippies schlepped in shit* for three days before they Saw The Light. Once back at their Park Avenue co-ops, they boosted some bread from their capitalist parents and bought up every Frye boot in Manhattan. **Note:** Jesus swung by Woodstock to check out Nirvanna. Nobody noticed Him. This explains why hippies smell that way: their clothing has been in a consignment shop for 2,000 years. P.S.: I wonder if the attendees at The Sermon On The Mount left behind as much unspeakable squalor and filth as the scumbags who attended Woodstock, The Isle of Wight, or any Earth Day/Antifa infestation.

*Those aging hippies better bring along Frye boots when visiting their grandchildren in LA or SF.

TPS: Gavin Newsome should walk the streets of San Francisco. In Birkenstocks. (This'll cure ya from "walkin in" your jeans, <u>pronto</u>.)

P.S.: "Birkenstock" is ancient Aramaic for "ain't getting' laid". Look it up.

GONNA WATCH CNN? I'LL SAVE YOU THE TROUBLE.

Collusion collusion collusion collusion collusion collusion racism racism racism racism racism racism racism recession recession recession recession recession recession.

P.S.: No one ever <u>hoped for</u> a recession before.

QUOTABLES

"Peace will come when Palestinians love their children more than they hate Israel."

-Golda Meir

"Divisiveness will end when Democrats love their Country more than they want to import unvetted, undocumented, unvaccinated, unskilled, unemployed Democrat voters."

-Golda Berto

"THE LUNACY OF FANATICS OF EVERY DENOMINATION HAS BEEN CALLED THE WILL OF GOD."*

A Jehovah's Witness's second-worst** nightmare is the Christian religions of the world firing their corrupt hierarchy, starting over on Bible-based terms, being of <u>some</u> Earthly assistance to each other (g-g-good works), and quietly worshiping God in harmony and grace, but <u>doing it on the wrong day</u>. The horror.

Note: No less an authority than St. Paul advised us to worship with friends regardless of the day they choose. Hmm. He may have been channeling a Big Guy, kind of a badass (cleared the Temple single-handedly) with a Spanish-sounding name who fired the Pharisees, abolished their Law, and sealed a New Covenant with his blood. Badass.

*<u>Kingdom of Heaven</u>, a Ridley Scott film.

**worst: an accountant escapes from their headquarters compound.

SF: MAYOR NEWSOME! A man just threw a drug syringe on the sidewalk!
GAVIN: Whew! I thought it was a plastic straw.

################
CELEBRATORY
CONSPIRACY CHAPTER
##################

FLAWED BUT NOT LAZY

Write political satire, be accused of arrogance. I will now begin every article with, "Yes, I am an asshole, but so is..." (James Clapper comes immediately to mind.)

DEATH WISH

The guy who heard Hillary say, "Kill them all," in Waco is still alive.....Sheeitt!* Scoff, sceptics, but if a six-foot sex pervert can hang himself form a five-foot bunk, this dude can shoot himself in the head and roll himself in a rug. Vince Foster proved this is possible back in the good old Whitewater days. Gun in the wrong hand? Check out the photos...What? No photos? Did you check the Rose Law Firm file?**

Q: Why'd the <u>Park Police</u> handle this?

A: Ask Hillary.

Q: How many homicides had the <u>Park Police</u> investigated?

A: None. "See? They needed the practice!" -HRC

Q: Why not view the negatives of the "lost" photos?

A: Polaroid cameras don't got no negatives. (Not even double ones. -Ed.)

Q: Why use a Polaroid camera?

A: <u>Polaroid cameras don't got no negatives.</u> (Am I going too fast for you?)

*Murderous Janet Reno obediently took "full responsibility"; your liberal compliant "news" media let it go. Seems them dead waifs weren't Mex-kin, so WAPO, The Grey Whore, and the Boston Gloat had no interest. **Note:** They cared not a whit when FBI tough guys shot a mother out from under the baby she was holding in her front doorway at Ruby Ridge, and no wonder. Mom was 'Merican, and conservative no less, as was her pre-teen son. We cannot confirm the political affiliation of the kid's dog, shot dead as well. Dammit, Janet.

**Caught ordering an aide to "vacuum the Rose Law Firm file", Hillary later alleged she said, "There is a vacuum in the Rose Law Firm file". Thus, a verb became a noun, and your fawning, dishonest mainstream media accepted this bullshit.

WHEN WILL THEY EVER LEARN? -Joan Baez, stealing someone else's shit.

Bill Mahr honestly (and stupidly) gave away Dem candidates' only chance to unseat Trump: recession recession recession (Repeat it enough and das volks vill believe it. -A. Hitler). They are rich enough to hedge against it, thinking they will reverse it when they regain power. Think again. Bernie's first step is to nationalize the oil industry. <u>That</u> primero pinito put pestoleum-rich Venezuela right back into the stone age. See: Gillibrand Glossary

Gillibrand Glossary: Socialist: a damn slow learner

(MORE) MY BABY DADDY vs TEEN MORON MOM

Ebonikasheeka will Fix Her Life. Three (3) men line up for tests to see which one be her baby daddy. This be on national TV (Oprah Channel) absent a hint of embarrassment, shame or remorse. If you be 14, you be knocked up. Any questions?

JIMMY KIMMEL MOCKS MELANIA'S 5th LANGUAGE ACCENT: zero to say on what passes for speech among those **born** here.

AGAINST ALL ODDS, BOTH WENT TO WASHINGTON: If Trump is the Davy Crockett of our time, Clinton is Jed Clampett.

GALA MISOGYN…MYSOGYN…SEXISM/ HOMOPHOBIA/FAKE NEWS SECTION

NOTICIA FALSA

Obama plays golf while Sandy devastates New Jersey. CNN: not a peep.

Trump plays golf while Dorian misses Florida. CNN: <u>all over</u> it.

ALL TALK

Q: What is one positive thing that Cory Booker ever did for Newark?

A: Shit. Still searchin' for sumpin' Elijah Cummings 'complished in Baltimore.

IT TAKES A VILLAGE

Work for a living: get drug tested.

Sit on your ass, collect food stamps/disability/energy assistance: huff away.

Note: Sport a neck tattoo and you may not get that job. Festoon yourself with total body ink and a pound o' piercings, why, you may waltz right into the welfare office and have an unelected career bureaucrat fawn over you while he/she/it signs you up for "entitlements" you never even <u>heard</u> of (Your 8 children share 3 phones just because they have different last names? Tsk, tsk. We'll fix <u>that</u>.) on the backs of the taxpayers.

Q: Why she don't care you spent thousands on body bling, ink, and you just put $5,000 worth of rims on your $500 ride?

A: Bro. Ain't <u>her</u> jack she be handin' out.

Next: Show your fake ID at the bar, not the voting booth. (That would be racist.)

CLOSET HETEROSEXUALS

At a Straight Pride Parade, Antifa thugs beat up paraders "to keep our community safe". If this makes sense to you, please vote Democrat. **Note:** AOC supports a bail bond fund for acts of violence committed against straight people. Congratulations liberals! You have created an environment which will get you hurt for publicly being not queer.

GILLIBRAND GLOSSARY

Women: A being, some say sentient, who overfills the garbage bag and acts astounded when you must remove some of the trash to tie it closed. This comes easy for her; she is, after all, capable of pretending to not know what partial-birth abortion entails. Onna plus side, she will **always** (sorry) leave you one (1) sheet of toilet paper. What a pal.

Note: By now, of course, you've switched to draw-string bags, which cost more but can be secured when overfilled. Have a heart and cut the loops: the animals at the dump are miserable enough without being lassoed by laziness and strangled by stupidity.

Speaking of stupidity: Att ladies and near-girls: keep buying Yoplait yogurt in those cutesy backward containers that were designed just for you, then go "Aw, poor thing" each and every time you see footage of baby skunks, squirrels, opossums, raccoons, etc. with their heads stuck in them, slowly suffocating to death. Damn dumbasses.

YOU HAVE A PROPERLY-STOCKED HOME when a hurricane warning is issued and you have to rush out and buy...nothing.

GALA ANIMAL WRONGS SECTION

PROVERBS 12:10

"Regarding" THE LIFE OF YOUR BEAST MEANS MORE THAN KEEPING IT ALIVE. Much more. Those who doubt this will be visited by something called "Karma". Pass it on.

EYES THAT SEE

Nursing a moribund animal? Photograph it every coupla days. The camera will see "Dad, I've had enough" about a week before you do.

YOUR WARM FUZZY IS NOT IN THEIR BEST INTEREST

A raccoon shows up so you put out food. Your un-immunized friend is soon joined by a skunk and an opossum. Bingo! You are now feeding wild animals. Rehab/relocation situation aside, this is indefensible. Reason 37: When you're gone, nature will efficiently and brutally restore the balance via starvation, predation and disease, which will be on YOU. Cumbaya.

Note: Sometimes death comes quickly. Feeding a Florida alligator (See Gator, Put Out Dog) will almost always get it shot, but at least it's quick. Cumbaya.

WALLY WORLD

Q: What causes "See Raccoon, Put Out Food" Syndrome?

A: Post WW II, an acid head/robber baron named Disney indoctrinated an entire generation with Bambi Brain, which anthropomorphizes animals, usually stopping just short of "See Cougar, Put Out Child" Syndrome. Cumbaya.

Q: What about "See Orca, Put Out Baby Baleen Whale" Syndrome?

A: Orcas don't eat baby whales, Silly; they drown them just for sport. Cumbaya.

Note: When bored with herding tuna, orcas are fond of hanging on the lower jaw of an adult baleen whale until it becomes exhausted, whereupon they eat its tongue and leave it to starve to death. Footage exists of a pod of orcas preventing a blue whale from sounding while their buddies chewed a door-sized hole in his side, again for sport. This frolic finally fatigued them, and the big guy swam off to a slow death by infection and starvation. Cumbaya.

Ps: Sharks kill to eat; never for sport. Hard to hate that. Orcas are a high order of intelligent mammals, and they are cruel bastards. ~~FREE~~ FUCK WILLY.

Finally, Orcas don't screw with sperm whales, whose bony heads make ballistic battering rams, as the crew in the whaling ship Essex found out. A sperm whale will head-butt an orca into hamburger, which sounds like a good use for them. Moreover, sperm whales have teeth, with which these badasses make a living eating Humboldt and giant squid. A yuppie broad once thought it was a Good Idea to swim with them. The sperm whales didn't. Cumbayaaah!

LIB-RALS ARE <u>TOLERANT</u>: Wear a plain red hat to class. Call me from the hospital.

HE…HE RENTED OUT A ROOM! Trump takes no salary. AOC may call him corrupt when she gives up hers.

FATHER MOTHER GOV-MINT KNOWS BEST SECTION

G ILLIBRAND GLOSSARY
Freedom (archaic): see "replaced by gov-mint"
Gov-mint: unelected career bureaucrats with "sociology" degrees in nothingness punch in and hit the cafeteria for a leisurely breakfast, except when the Weather Channel advises "all non-essential gov-mint employees" to stay home.
Non-essential gov-mint employee (redundant): see "sociology major".

A.O.C. WORLD

2017: Gov-mint mandates corkscrew light bulbs; they have mercury but save lectric.

2018: Gov-mint forbids corkscrew light bulbs; they save lectric but have mercury.

COLLUSION MEETS PER DIEM, CAUSES COW FARTS -The New York Times

Q: CNN said soldiers stay at the Trump Turnberry rather than the Hyatt. Why?

A: To save $20 a night. (This obstructs collusion and causes recession. -AOC)

SHOOT THE DEER, NOT THE (NEW GREEN) DEERE

An alumnus of the Michael Belliselles Graduate School of Tenured Hoaxes became alarmed upon hearing of a .50 caliber thingie that is spot-on accurate and therefore dangerous. (yes, he said that.) The piece turned out to be a muzzle loading rifle which, like the caliber .50 Browning Machine Gun and its derivatives, has a half-inch hole in its barrel. Lengthwise. At this point, similarities dwindle, but I appreciate the man-bun's concern about its accuracy. We all want a weapon which, when aimed at a woodchuck, shoots out the tractor tire instead, but we <u>should not be allowed</u>. Tractors have rights, too.

NEW GREEN RULES FOR SELF-DEFENSE

"You must match force with an equal level of force." -Cumbaya crowd

You awake to find a burglar in your home. She brandishes a club. You haul out a handgun. Realizing that you will be arrested rather than the home invader, you pitch your pistol out the window and deploy your daughter's baseball bat*. The thug grabs a Glock from her waistband and points it at your nutsack. Now, don't YOU feel like a fucking asshole?

*Your girl plays softball, soccer, lacrosse, and football.

Your boy plays Dungeons & Dragons. Advantage: progressives.

NO MEN ALLOWED

Swear to God, the major league baseball announcer said, "No runs, 2 hits, and 2 people left on base". How ridiculous! He could just as easily have said, "No runs, 2 hits, amd 2 persons who identify with the male gender (at the moment) left on base". What is <u>wrong</u> with him?

AIN'T PUSHIN NO BUTTON <u>TWICE</u>! Leave the house and trust a timer to keep the dryer from burning the place down.

BAD TRADE

AOC wants fewer cows, more indigents. Hmm. Cows fart, but they don't shit on sidewalks, toss diapers and syringes out of car windows, or burglarize, rob or rape anybody. **Plus,** indigent immigrants help the environment by signing up for every freebie their native hellhole could not provide, thus bankrupting their host country (that would be US). Factories close, fossils fuels remain buried, and the air gets real clean ('cept, of course, for that shit on a hot sidewalk smell). No can pay that pesky mortgage? !No te preoccupes! Your govmint now provides free tents, water, and since this may depress you, free needles. You may now join the rats and vagrants in any Democrat-run sanctuary city. Yay.

FROM TOP TO BOTTOM

Always guessed that him-ish Hillary was a top? Guess again.

1- Bill publicly humiliated her via liaisons with trailer park trash.
2- A political outsider with "no chance" defeated her.
3- She pretended to be President in a photo shoot.

<u>Do the math</u>. The broad's a masochist.

TV SHOW SYNOPSES

Adam Ruins Everything

1- Rodeo is a Spanish word so we should give Texas back to Mexico.
2- Everything the United States has done/is doing/will ever do is evil.

CNN "News"

1- Collusion/Obstruction/recession/hotel room renting/Melania wore high heels.

2- Everything the United States has done/is doing/will ever do is evil.

HAPLESS, GUTLESS AND IMPOTENT

When Obama's top law enforcement, Attorney General Corrupt Eric Holder, refused to disclose why his boneheaded Fast and Furious gun control scheme got a border patrol agent killed <u>and</u> placed thousands of guns in the hands of drug cartel thugs, your United States Congress held him in contempt.

Q: What does it mean when you are held in contempt of Congress?

A: Nothin'

OOPS

Dried out the pork roast? Pour an inch of apple juice over it and cover. 'Bout an hour it'll plump right up. Next day: nice sammiches. -Betty Berto

MIRROR

"We are all made in God's image and likeness." -Sister St. John-of-the-Holy-Cross

"Christ, He sure is letting Himself go lately." -Philbertio Excommunicatio

WHY DOES THE FARM BUREAU PRINT A MENU? It's **gonna** be pulled pork, butter beans, cream corn, sweet tea, 'nanna pudding. And Wonder bread.

SATURDAY MORNIN', COMIN' DOWN -Johnny (Kris) Berto

Review: <u>National Sunday Law</u> by A. Jan Marcussen

In 1982, when this book was written, it was still thought that our gov-mint could 'complish something. We now know it can't secure our borders or arrest Madonna for threatening to bomb the White House. Curiously, people still read Marcussen, whose main premise is that mainstream evangelical Christians will pressure the gov-mint to force everybody to worship God every single Sunday. He cares not a whit that gov-mint might meddle in religion; his only concern is that it might be done contrary to the concepts conjured by his chosen cult.

1- In the aeons B.T. (before Trump), evangelicals couldn't prevail on the gov-mint to stop funding abortion mills like Planned Parenthood who routinely suck the brains out of babies after they are old enough to cry. Case fucking closed.

2- C'mon, let's beat this dead horse. The book ably points out the corruption that quickly enveloped the original Christian Church, Catholicism. Those who broke away during the Reformation eliminated many of the abuses; most managed to maintain the quaint tradition of torturing dissidents to death. John Calvin would burn you alive for translating the bible into German so folks could **read** it; C of E was happy to murder you for teaching your kids the Lord's prayer in English. Heretic! Many came to America to escape religious persecution so they could enthusiastically practice it.

3- We are reminded that Saturday worship was moved to Sunday to facilitate fraternizing with and then c-c-converting buncha pagans who were accustomed to schmoozing the sun god on a Sun-day. (Moon-god: Mon-day) Anyone who has seen the Best Baptist Church empty out and hotfoot overt The Smokin' Pig BBQ Emporium before those Church of God apostates tie up the buffet line (You think I am making this up, don't you?) knows how compelling Sun-day rituals can be. For early Christians, this was a two-fer (also available at The Smokin' Pig) in that it also helped sever ties with Judaism, itself never quite the same since some Spanish* Guy fires the Pharisees, overrules their Law, and punches the pilot on the flight into Egypt...but that's another story. *Well, His <u>name</u> was Spanish...

4- 'Nother sop to the pagans was to allow graven images. They hada change the Commandments for this, ending up with that illogical split of the 10th just to maintain, well, 10. (Can you picture Charlton Heston a-comin' down the mountain with 9 Commandments? Neither could they.) Now, 'steada stuff you'd spy through the smoke in any aging hippie's bedroom, the hierocrats hauled in statues of saints, much as we had monuments of our war heroes until "liberals" started pulling them down. (Hmmm. Wonder if Warren will have us burning books again.) Anyway, we are supposed to care about this supposed travesty.

Bottom line: per Marcussen's musing, what a great victory for Satan a National Sunday Law would have been! Imagine the entire world ('cept them damn Jews) fervently worshipping the same God every damn Sunday. The horror! Has our society not fallen apart at the hands of feminists, progressives, and other so-called liberals, we might coulda had lotsa folks a-churchin' of a Saunday, then having a quiet family gathering at the park or in the backyard absent lawn-mowers, weedeaters, and yes, chainsaws stealing their peace. When Jehova's Witnesses proved powerless to stave off the calamity of quiet Sundays, the dissolution of the family handled it for them. Yay.

God must be grateful for this happy outcome. Now, all He has going on is Islamists taking over where the old-time "Christians" left off by burning people to death, throwing them off buildings, drowning them in cages, etc. Compared to such child's play, He almost had to face having His entire creation (except them damn Jews) worship-ping Him in quiet, loving harmony <u>on the wrong fucking day</u>. He has to be relieved that it never happened. Now, as for Satan, well, she must be sooo pissed.

THE DIFFERENCE BETWEEN the Best Baptist and the reg-lar Baptist church: newer cars, real Rolexes.

MORRIS CHRIST

A Jew I once worked for was a gentleman in every way, including the fact that he rarely swore. When he did, his chosen expletive, invariably, was, "Jesus Christ!" No matter how sideways the situation, the irony of that epithet always made me laugh. I am confident he knew why.

BAG LIMIT

Q: How many rape-murders will Montgomery County cover up before it starts turning illegal immigrant felons over to ICE?

A: 'Slong as they're spread out to one a week (8 so far), prob'ly all of them. (10 as of 9/20/19)

COOL LIGHTING

Q: Where do moviemakers find light bulbs that clank when turned on?

A: On motorboats that have no neutral, which is where they keep bolt action rifles that make lever action sounds. (Movie folks don't get out much.)

USEFUL IDIOTS

Radical environmentalists are good for the economy. A city employee told the recycling commandant that he had a use for some chain link fencing that had been dropped off. "We're recycling that!", she shrieked, blocking her treasure with her torso until it could be mechanically loaded, transported by road and rail to a steel mill, melted in a coal-fired furnace, poured into pigs, beaten into billets, rolled into rods, drawn into wire, and manufactured into...why, chain link fencing. Thank ~~God~~ Earth Mother he wasn't permitted to pitch it into his pickup, drive it home, and r-r-reuse it. Cumbaya.

PASEO DEL PADRE

"Divisive rhetoric" is closemindedliberal code for how meanspirtedrepublicans, particularly Trump, inartfully describe the real world. Meanwhile, the cumbaya crowd want to punch the President in the face (DeNero), shoot him

(Depp), bomb the White House (Madonna), display his severed head (Griffin), and stab him to death (Shakespeare in the Park). Trust you local Archbishopric to derogate the former and ignore the latter. No surprise there; priests parse preaching to preserve paying parishioners. Lotsa prattle 'bout funding idleness and rewarding indolence (St. Paul's caveat about "no workee, no eatee"* be damned) while tepidly skirting the greatest evil of our time. During his vaunted visit to the U.S., the Pope gave it seven (7) words. "Life is precious in all its forms."** is the closest Il Papa, chief pretender among those who fancy themselves descendants of the Apostles of The Lion of Judah, came to condemning the current holocaust. All the philosophical platitudes about life beginning at conception ignore the obvious distinction that terminating a not-yet viable life is less monstrous than late-term/partial-birth abortion, which murders babies when they are developed enough to cry.

*old orthodox Aramaic. Look it up.

**We learned <u>that</u> in Boy Scouts, priest.

Excommunicatio celerito: How many unvetted unvaccinated unemployed indigent illegal invading aliens has Your Excellency smuggled into **his** neighborhood?

IT'S A TEST

McCormick markets tiny vials of vanilla for $3.96; any Cuban bodega stocks quart bottles for two bucks.

################
PROSCRIBED BY
POCAHONTAS SECTION
######################

AS YUPPIES (CHICKS <u>AND</u> MAN-BUNS) SAY: EEEUUU!
Older cats often develop allergies which can cause "chin acne", sometimes spreading to their face between eyes and ears. Itches like a bitch. Apoquel helps, as does mild debridement with a toothbrush.

Q: You buy a toothbrush for a <u>cat?</u>

A: Heavens, no. My wife has a frequent guest I am not overly fond of.

HELLO, USEFUL IDIOTS. MY NAME IS...

My name is Pete. I have a husband, and I'm running for President.*

My name is Beto. I'm taking anything that functions like granddads duck gun.

My name is Pliz. I'm gonna raise your taxes to pay for those who don't pay any.

My name is Castro.** I "list" any American who dares disagree on anything.

Note: If any of this shit "energizes" you, <u>please</u> vote Democrat.

*Lifted straight from, "I'm so relieved. I am now the <u>second</u>-worst President.

Roz, thank Barack for me."

**There are 3 of these devils if you count Fidel; 4 considering Che.

OLYMPIC COMMITTEE: NEW TEST (or ASK ANY JUDGE)

When told to raise her right hand in court, there is a 50-50 chance that a woman will do so. (The odds improve if her left arm is missing.)

Q: Must there **Always** be a toxic feminity section?

A: Only until the other 60% wear the right size.

Q: What's <u>that</u> have to do with 70% pay?

A: It means it's 30% too high. (100 minus 60 equals 40% Get It Right, <u>and they wear it</u>. Imagine them specin' out an aircraft carrier:

Him: Uh, it was supposed to be 1,000' long.

Her: Well, it's 400'. Deal with it. (Hear me roar.)

P.S.: "We are responsible for the effort, not the results." -any lib-ral

"Tell that to your surgeon." -any sentient being

WHAT THEY GONNA DO? CRUCIFY HIM?

Coupla thousand years ago, a big carpenter's apprentice steps up, takes off His tool belt, tugs Caiaphas' sleeve, and tells him that he (Caiaphas) is so caught up in the letter of the Law that he has lost its purpose, and asks him (Caiaphas) if he agreed that what we <u>do</u> is more important than what we say. He (Caiaphas) didn't.

P.S.: Caiaphas went on the found the "faith only" faction, which is alive and well in many "Christian" churches. All he hada do is cherry-pick St. Paul, ignore The Sermon on the Mount, and disregard The Man's <u>actions</u> throughout His entire blessed life. Kin Ah git uh A-men?

Q: IF ELECTED, WILL WARREN BURN BUNCHA BOOKS?

A: How ridiculous! That's Amazon, Google, and Facebook's job.

CALIFORNIA DREAMIN'

You want a new tattoo but the rent is doo. Go get your sleeve, Sis; add some fresh piercings while you're attit. Celebrate your new-found beauty with a carton o' ciggie-butts and a case of beer. Onna way home, get on your gov-mint giveaway "free" phone and call the nearest unelected career bureaucrat to claim mold in your rent-assisted (at taxpayer expense) apartment. You'll have a year while they "process" your claim; meanwhile, the owner will be powerless to collect rent or evict you. Congratulations! You just a got a year's "free" rent and a nice new tatt (plus some fresh body bling) on the back of some working stiff. You are now a Democrat for life, and you didn't even have to be snuck into the Country by a drug/human trafficking cartel. Yay.

P.S.: This is a win-win for you and Kamala Harris; both of you have no shame.

Gillibrand glossary "free": purchased with O.P.M (Other People's Money) see: "Democrat")

REAL NEWS, FAKE NEWS, AND REAL FAKE NEWS

Callow cub reporter: Hunter Biden sold us out to China <u>and</u> Ukraine?

Old CNN hand: Son, the <u>story</u> is that Trump tried to find out if Hunter Biden sold us out to China and Ukraine. He may have <u>asked</u> someone.

Cubbie: So...so what was Hillary's uranium deal with Russia?

Handjob: Why, that was no story at all.

EQUAL OPPORTUNITY ANNOYER

Q: By their own stats, 60% of women wear the wrong pad. Do men wear the wrong cup?

A: Hey, I...I <u>need</u> a large. No more questions!

OATMEAL VS HAM & EGGS

Q: What's the easiest way to stop eating greasy food?

A: Angina.

BENEFULOSHIT AND BONG HITS

Hey Moe! Let's artificially dye the dog & cat food we sell to the commune crowd to remind them we put veggies in their **carnivore** feed. We'll save on meat and them ex-hippies'll think they're saving the planet*. Cumbaya.

*They can't possibly think their **carnivore** <u>wants</u> peas & carrots.

*****

BARTENDER, I'LL HAVE A VODKA/NITRO, PLEASE

Nitroglycerine didn't touch it; just in time I realized I was suffering from alcohol deprivation. Thank you, Jesus. Now I can finish wri... ______________

"CUT" OR "MOW"?

You know she's cheating when she says, "I have a...a person coming over to cut the lawn".

ONNA PLUS SIDE, THEY NEVER POOP WHERE YOU STEP

I understand wanting a change of scenery, but why the urgency? I'm in the middle of takin' a bath when the cat 'bout knocks the door down tryin' to get in. When he tires of watching the big whatever splash around, he wants back out. <u>Now</u>. Same when he chooses to go out on the porch, or come in from the porch. He has an agenda which is far more important than anything I have going on.

I finally sat him down for a talk. "Bro", says I, "you're a <u>cat</u>. You are not going to accomplish <u>anything</u> today. Or tomorrow. Or the next day. <u>It doesn't matter</u> whether you do nothing on the porch, or if you do nothing on the couch, or if you do nothing in the kitchen. Now stop bugging me."

He looked at me as if to say, "So, exactly what are **you** going to achieve today?". He had a point.

SIGNS

"I have a...a person coming over to fix the framistan." -She's seeing someone.

"That's was fun! See you next Tuesday. How 'bout late AM?" -She's seeing someone.

"Wow! You are simply The Best! Don't forget to pay me." -She's supporting someone.

Note: If she dances on tables, her hero is some deadbeat. Every time.

SAVE THE ENVIRONMENT: DIAPER THE ENVIRONMENTALISTS

Q: Who leaves behind more unspeakable filth: the Woodstock generation, Earth Day dreamers, Antifa thugs, or climate change alarmists?

A: 'Bout the same. The sheer volume of trash strewn by these pigs constitutes vandalism, not free speech. Luckily, in sanctuary cities, Democrat machine politics have ordered things so when these slobs come through, why, you'd hardly notice.

P.S.: Mixed with folks following Federal freebies are hardworking people who came to this Country to escape the violence and filth of their native hellholes. Seeing the squalor of sanctuary cities must make them wonder why they bothered.

MAINTENANCE ~~MAN~~ PERSON

Unscrew* the kitchen faucet aerator. Put a large pot inna sink to reduce splashing. Open both valves <u>fully</u> for 10 seconds. Look at what's in the pot. Reverse the process after backwashing the aerator.

Note: Do this quarterly and you won't be boiling your pasta in pipe mung.

*Ladies: lefty-loosie. (Watch which hand they raise on Judge Judy. It's the other one.) Man-buns: Keep doing what the girls do.

PROVERBS 12:10 (AGAIN)

If you feed a bit later in summer when it's a little cooler, remember to adjust this forward in fall as the days get shorter. Bad shit happens when domestic animals are fed late. **Glossary:** sand colic: Southern for, "My horse is trying to stay alive on worn-out pasture/my front yard because $20 worth of feed frightens me". See: "Can't feed 'em? Don't breed 'em!" Dumbass.

WHISTLEBLOWER CIRCLE JERK

"My information is hearsay but it must be true because the media reported it." Huh?

PRIORITIES

Dwight D. Eisenhower was visiting his Gettysburg farm. His aides gasped when a spirited colt slipped his halter and began frolicking on a newly-installed putting green. Finally someone spoke. "Isn't that a wonderful sight", said the President.

THINK

Cut anything that has a loop before throwing it out so it doesn't end up around and animal's neck at the landfill. Dump dwellers' lives are miserable enough, second only to those in sanctuary cities. If you toss fishing line or nets without cutting them up, you are a criminal. P.S.: Your tackle shop has a device that cuts old line right on the reel. It falls off into harmless pieces. For that service you may pay a buck more for new line (The horror!), but you'll leave with the latest tips on what and where. Do-dah.

FUNDAMENTALISM MEETS JUDGEMENTALISM

The nuns took entire classes to the theater to protest because the name sounded disrespectful. Then someone on staff snuck out and <u>saw</u> the thing. A year later, Jesus Christ Superstar was the subject of parochial school plays across the Country. Amen. **Note:** In the movie version, Pilate touched Jesus after the scourging. As he condemns Christ, a huge glass bowl is brought out. The procurator thrusts his hands into it; the water turns blood red. Kinda gets your attention.

P.S.: 'Bout here's where your fundamentalist friend'll offer: "Thee Babble don't sigh they were no glay-iss bowl, nohow". Way-ell, thee Babble don't sigh they weren't none, nay-ther.

CALL ME MR. ~~TIBBS~~ DEMOCRAT

They crave open borders, unfettered immigration from terrorist states (<u>more</u> Omars?), and no ICE. They revel in every American fault and refuse to acknowledge any American virtues. They hate half the Country (deplorables) and resist the will of the people when it fails to agree with their radical agenda. To unseat an elected President who will be <u>voted on</u> in one (1) year, they call on "patriotism" to impeach him. Gimme a break.

Note: Three generations of piss-poor parenting (put down the bong, Gramma) and NEA (union, no competency testing) teaching have first dumbed-down and then indoctrinated our kids to the point that the survival of this Country is now in doubt. This is not "patriotism". This is subversion.

BRAVE NEW BIOLOGY

The Boy Scouts of America got an annual contribution and were in my will. Now that they are the Boy/Girl/Undecided Scouts: nope.

Q: When can a teen transvestite join the Girl Scouts?

A: Any time it wants to. (politically correct answer: any time they* want to.)

* "they": he/she/it/undecided

SCOUTMASTER

Gays never use positions of authority to get over on kids. Ask any coach, sports doctor, or priest.

LADIES LAIR

The old man goin' fishin' 'steada friskin' ya?

Watchin' foot ball but won't give ya a foot rub?

Bookin' the spread 'steada spreadin' your book?

<u>Look to your fragrance</u>. If he wanted to smell that flowery shit you're wearin', he'd go to a viewing. This might be a good time to pitch some new additions to the Get Lucky Line. Our original offerings of Just -In Motorcycle Tires,

Just-Fired Shotgun Shell, and Just-Worn High Heels are now augmented by Just-Got- Here Pizza, Just-Poured Beer, and Just-Baked Bread*. Coming soon: Pizza/Beer/Sweaty Girl, A Blend (includes morning-after pill). Do-dah.

*Some of you already have this covered.

DO THEM A FAVOR: TAKE THEM TO SUITABLE HABITAT AND <u>LEAVE THEM ALONE</u>

Finding the outside cat dish overturned? 'Possum (or armadillo). Dish upright but filthy? 'Possum (or armadillo). 'Dillos, you see, grub for...grubs. Their marsupial mates are omnivorous, which includes carrion. This 'splains* why they become unkempt as teenagers and smell real bad as adults, and they don't even do meth. While no baby elephants, young opossums are (unlike their parents) not unlovely, but they eat dead stuff, sometimes old dead stuff. Like buzzards, they have a natural immunity to bad bacteria, but do your domestic animals? Do you? Your best move is to trap 'em and deport 'em (don't tell no lib-rals) to an undeveloped area having a perennial pond or stream and a fair-sized woodlot ('Possums prefer spending time aloft for scouting/security/safe sex. <u>Let</u> 'em.)

Omnivorous: means it eats any damn thing. See also: Cajun

*cultural appropriation courtesy of Desi Arnaz (R.I.P.). Fucking sue me.

P.S.: Adult opossums don't run; they waddle. If you are among the louts who run them (and turtles, snakes, etc.) over because you can, you are in for some unpleasantness. Think today's "liberal" thought police are vicious? Wait 'till you see what Karma has in store for you. Mindlessly murdering the Lord's innocents <u>will</u> piss Him off. Dumbass.

HOW THEY MAKE FAKE NEWS

We put together a newsroom to conjure Russian collusion. It did a wonderful job. We are now doing the same for obstruction and recession. -NYT

ps: Lewandowski was snide; Strzok wasn't. (Even Wolf laughed at that one.)

UKRAINE'S PRESIDENT offered the skinny on Biden corruption. We don't want that. Trump accepted the info and asked for more. We want that. It was about the 2016 election, but we'll morph it into the 2020 campaign. Watch this: "Trump can't win an election without foreign meddling". -CNN

"AFTER MY THREAT TO withhold funds, they fired their AG in six hours." -Joe Biden

"Trump acts like a mafia boss." -MSNBC

HILLARY DESTROYED 30,000 E-mails, swiped servers, smashed cell phones. Trump provided a transcript, not a recording. He's not transparent. -MEDIA MOB

TEENS DON'T GET ROOMS

I am old enough to remember when safe sex meant parking where the police wouldn't find ya.

PHYSICIAN, HEAL THYSELF

Veterinarian: Kinda like a doctor for animals, except that he/she still knows how to bandage, diagnose a patient*, and keep a fucking appointment.

Doc Vet does this all day long with patients who can't say where it hurts.

Q: Where do you take vegans when they get sick?

A: A botanist.

Q: Who does a Christian Scientist with appendicitis see?

A: His Maker.

PICKIN' YER HIS-TRY

European-American settlers' treatment of Native Americans was generally unfair and often brutal; they were sometimes as sadistic towards native peoples as were the Indians to the settlers (and each other). Nowhere were indigenous people subjected to greater abuse than in the Spanish colonies, which were a study in subjugating natives by viciously eradicating their culture for commercial and, of course, religious reasons.

Q: What will my teacher or professor* say about Spanish atrocities?

A: ¿Que?

*see: tenured hoax

THE POOR DUMB BASTARD

He took her off the street, cleaned her up (adult clothing, makeover, toenail trim, flea dip, etc.), built them a home, and m-m-married her. A year later he asked that she save the garbage can for stinky stuff and leave big, clean things like water jugs (which he recycled) 'longside.

Q: What did it mean when she persisted?

A: Meant she'd be getting the house, the car, and half his pension*

*the poor, dumb bastard.

THEY HATE U.S. THAT MUCH...

Trump was turning around 8 years worth of damaged American prestige and achieving some tight trade deals, so the Democrats put their own Country at risk, struck with Strzok, Brennan, Clapper et al and timed their tantrums to torpedo talks with North Korea and China in a desperate attempt to deny Trump a success.* Democrat-compliant CNN colluded by airing every fatuous allegation just as Air Force 1 alighted on foreign soil. Yay.

*When collusion fails, try obstruction. Nothing there? Simply repeat "recession" until people believe there is one. Not happening? Aw, just go right to impeachment.

Q: Why don't Dems let The People decide next election?

A: 'Cause The People may not vote "correctly", Silly.

ps: At least Dems don't want to open our borders to needy people a/k/a guaranteed Democrat voters...Oops! Will our taxes go up to pay for more parasites? Per Liz P. Fleming Warren: "Grbl fzzz mljhgx dvptc flpzd".

LGBT/WHAT-<u>EVER</u>: The butch was the "wife". Is the fem the "husband"? I'm confused. (**Editor:** <u>You're</u> confused?)

LIONS AND TIGERS AND BEARS, OH MY!

A foreign gov-mint helped Trump track Biden, Brennan, and Clapper corruption. Uh, yup, and the po-lice often call Interpol. What's your point there, Sparky?

CATS

Delusional Cat Owner: Spunk, you're gonna hafta move.

Spunk: Meow meow meow me meow meow meow. (<u>You're</u> gonna hafta change your plans.)

Note: Animal rights Nazis and other "liberals" would ban the "owner" reference.

Hot Tip: If I'm buyin' the food, scoopin' the shit, and payin' the vet, I'll call myself the "owner". If "lib-rals" prevail in 2020, this <u>will</u> get me arrested. While imprisoned for word infraction, AOC will come to my home to feed the cat, scoop the poop, pay the vet, etc. Ain't Democrats wonderful?

Ps: Spunk is a pussy cat...I mean, she identifies with the female cat gender. For now. Surely some product of public school indoctrination at Pampered Pussy Boarding will advise her, maybe even pressure her, to choose a different gender "assignment". Ain't lib-rals wonderful? Should she decline, Spunk will be bussed to Yale*University, shoved into a safe space, and reeducated about the error of her thought. Aint progressives wonderful?

*Yale, where students protested a Free Speech lecture (You think I am making this up, don't you?). "I guess they missed the irony class", said Charlie Kirk, author of <u>Campus Battlefield</u>.

RATS

Republicans are hapless, gutless, and stupid. Democrats are shrewd, sneaky, and ruthless, willing to sacrifice the good of their own Country for political gain. Advantage: Democrats. So why won't they win in 2020? Why, because they can't count. They have locked up the LGBT/WHATEVER, Antifa, and Malcontent Living In Mommy's Basement (as we said. Antifa) vote. Put another way, they have made loyal, lifelong Democrat voters out of 10% of the population.

Q: Doesn't this piss off the other 90%?

A: Only those whose taxes are used to fund crap they abhor like Planned Parenthood.

Q: Conservative tax dollars should not fund an abortion mill?

A: Only when lib-ral tax dollars fund the NRA.

IMITATED BUT NOT FLATTERED

Seeking to stoke(ly) the race hustling/victimization genre, Sharpton's secretary whined, "Whites don't appreciate black culture until they adopt it". He's right*. Until their teenager's third breeding by three dif-rent baby daddy, why, most white folk don't think 'bout black culture at all.

*Not a typo. See? You lib-rals cling to the secretary = chick cliché. Who are the sexists here?

SHE HAS DONE EVERYTHING in her power to make herself look like a man, but calls herself the "wife". Her feminine partner is the "husband". If this makes sense to you, so will Elizabeth Fleming Warren being called a "person of color" by a university president. Please vote Democrat. Dumbass.

TELL ME AGAIN

Q: Who thought Elizabeth Fleming Warren was a "person of color"?

A: Ray Charles.

"...GOD MEND THINE EVERY FLAW..."*

Older blacks know that you never owned a slave, nor did your daddy, or your grand daddy, or your great...you get the picture. Workingmen and women, black and white, have been busting their asses for generations. This escapes today's young punks, who are far more caught up in the slavery issue than their elders ever were, nevermind that they are yet one more (privileged) generation removed from that horror.

Q: Why are today's kids so quick to play the slavery victimization card?

A: Indoctrination by lib-ral NEA (union, no competency testing) teachers.

Suggestion: Monitor a class someday. All the wonderful accomplishments of your Country will be ignored while each hateful act is showcased by people who would not interrupt their jogging to help an old lady cross the street.

*from a patriotic song called "America The Beautiful", which your kids have never heard. Thank a teacher.

Gillibrand glossary: patriotic: xenophobic, sexist, racist, probably pro-NRA.

YUPPIE BROAD

"I don't want to hear that you buy bottled water!", she kvetched, putting her hands to her ears (Swear to God). I then expected her to hold her breath and stamp her feet, but she followed with, "Haven't you heard of Brita?". Lessee. I drink spring water, which has minerals Brita cannot add to city water. Oh, and I recycle the bottles and every glass, steel, and aluminum container I use. Bitch is bothered by bottles, but throws every damn thing inna trash. I'd offer to compare carbon footprints with her, but then I'd sound like Al Private Jet/ Five-House Gore. P.S.: Don't nobody got laid that night.

VEGANS WALK THE WALK

Yuppies get their burger in little square packages while disparaging those nasty hunters. News flash: If you buy meat, someone else does your killing for you. I challenge you to eat one (1) wild game meal, preferably from a hoofed animal, and feed Fido* the leftovers. Next day, you and your canine friend will feel and act years younger. The strength of that noble creature will brace your body; its courage will help heal your sorry soul. No wonder Indians thanked their kills.

P.S.: Won't be no fat, so braise coupla bone-in pieces <u>rare</u> for your domestic carnivore, then watch her eat. From a distance.

*Louisiana: Phideaux

I HATE TRUCK RACING

Hey Moe! Let's race something that is patently unsuited to the task.

Q: You mean, bowl race a pickup truck?

A: Don't be ridiculous. Let's at least use a shopping cart.

Truck racing encourages young snotty to install loud pipes (and little else) on his 4 wheeled shoebox and be a nuisance around town.

Q: What do you tell a punk who revs his engine when he sees other guys?

A: "Just keep thinkin' you're straight."

ATT FOX NEWS: I THINK Wilford Brimley in Absence of Malice is really John Durham when he was fat.

####################
CLOSET HETEROSEXUAL
SECTION
####################

COBBLER CAPITALISM

Somebody should make women's shoes that run crazy-large. That way, Miss Thing can shove her size 10 hoofs into 'em and say she wears a 6. They'll sell a crapload. **Note:** makers of horse jockey boots already do this to help the lads with their resume' stats.

P.S.: Wanna buy her some sexy shoes but don't know her size? <u>Ask* her.</u> "These are 6 ½" means she found the only 6.5s on the planet that fit. She wears a 7. (Not open toe? 7 ½.)

*Better yet, offer to take her shopping (100% she'll go) and wander into a ladies' shoe store. You slip every pair on and off her. This is a twofer:

1- pisses off every married woman whose husband can't spell Charles Jourdan;

2- you find out early in the game if she has gnarly feet.

CHILDREN OF THE CHILDREN OF THE FLOWER CHILDREN:
HOW THE 1960s RUINED A COUNTRY

The microwave instructions end with, "Contents will be hot". Your kids <u>need</u> this. Thank any NEA (union, no competency testing) teacher and yourself, plus your own bong-huffing progenitrix and <u>her</u> hippie (Gramma's goin' clear again!) Sanctity of Motherhood. Peace.

AYE, MATEY: CAN-YA CAPITALISM (might be a good time to buy W. Grant & Sons stock)

Our Nicaraguan friends have long made a fine dark rum picturesquely named Flor de Cana. Their light libation, Extra Secco, is 'bout as smooth as Bacardi Superior but has more flavor. Curiously, when mixed with Coke, the taste goes away to the point that you'll go 50/50 before you've mixed a drink that'll get you a compliment. Remember this next time you feel piratical towards M'Lady. **N.B.:** keep track o' your glass, son. As always, the goal is to get <u>her</u> to make rash decisions, not you. ARRGH! Importer: William Grant & Sons, New York

Buzzkill: even if she signed a release or got <u>you</u> drunk and had her way with <u>you</u>, it don't make no nevermind. "A woman must be believed", says Kirsten Gillibrand, and all our lib-ral friends will nod their empty heads and chant: "#Me Too Pulled A Train In High School". Thirty-six (36) years from now, tearfully and in baby talk, bitch <u>will</u> accuse you of rape. Hear me roar.

WE WON! THE PEOPLE HAVE SPOKEN! WE LOST. THE PEOPLE ARE DEPLORABLE

Populist: What Democrats proport to be when We The People vote "liberal"*.

Socialist: What Democrats become when We The People vote conservative.

*"liberal" is in quotes because it now means the opposite. See: Red Hat Test.

NO WORRIES

Not sure what she'll do while you're out of town? Buy her buncha chocolate bars before you go. From what I've seen in the Lindt ads, she'll never leave the house.

P.S.: Did I pull my card too soon? "You're good", said the cute CVS cashier; then her eyes went back to all that chocolate. Her expression changed to: "Apparently not".

LEXI-CON

at CNN, The President of The United States is "Trump": a high school class skank is always "Dr. Ford".

THEY HAVE...CONNECTIONS

You don't pray TO them; you ask for their help. Still, lotsa folks deny the intercession of saints. I doubted, too, until Dad (who was no saint) helped me with a project. (He was a master carpenter; I hammer nails.) As I built something I was never trained for, I wondered: "How did I know how to do that?"* More recently, an outside cat came home from St. Vetrix wearing a C-collar. Hada keep him inside 'till the stitches came out. He spent 3 days under the bed and hardly ate. Onna 4th I told Francis and Anthony they were doing a crappy job, whereupon Cat emerged, ate, and hopped up <u>on</u> the bed. See? Even saints need some straightening-out once in a while.

*Sure, Jesus prob'ly had a hand in it; I've heard He was a pretty good apprentice, although His forte' was, like, Bible study and such.

P.S.: I put a graven image of Dad on my desk. Jesus already had the wall.

THEY <u>CONCERNED</u> BOUTCHA

Inna South, folks from the next town look where they going (Bless they hearts). Neighbors peer into you propitty as they drive by. Hope they don't wreck. Too badly.

P.S.: Minding your own damn business is not "unfriendly". Y'all.

HEAR ME ROAR

Madonna would bomb the White House without a care for all the innocents who work there. American women still swoon.

Kathy Griffith holds a facsimile of the severed head of The President of The United States, whom half the Country elected. American women still support this troll's "comeback".

Jane Fonda sat in the gunner's seat of a North Vietnamese anti-aircraft piece pretending to shoot down their sons. American women still bought Hanoi Jane's fucking workout video.

Pardon me while my misogyny metastasizes.

P.S.: The V.F.W. (still) has urinal deodorant pucks featuring Fonda's face. Cool.

SOCIALISTS <u>SEEK</u> SECOND-BEST

You've dispensed with Dad and celebrate single moms. Meanwhile, your daughter is knocked-up, your son can't hang a shelf, your 8-month old is in day-care, and you still rent. What else has progressivism done for you? Sure, there are Moms who can teach their boy to hunt, fish, fire a snot rocket, and write his name in the snow, but it's like buying booze from a Baptist: it just doesn't <u>feel</u> right.

Q: What do you say to a young man who played video games instead of sports?

A: "Oh, waitress!"

CLEAN MEAT BEATS BIG PHARMA

Fed the dog game meat every other day and halved her arthritis meds.

Q: How'd you get her off the other half?

A: Fed her game meat every day.

P.S.: Her step ramp is now shed siding. Do-dah.

<u>REALLY</u> WHITE PRIVILEGE

Elizabeth P. Fleming Warren has to <u>make up</u> adversity in her life. It must be nice.

##############################

SEXISM ALERT

##############################

Q UIDADO QUE TE CREIA

"There are Jews, Mr. President, and there are Jews." – Henry Kissinger

"There are Southerners, and there are Northfloridians." -P.Phantomini

Like you, onliest thing I knew about Richard Nixon (today it's the NRA and Trump) was what biased, dishonest, liberal-compliant "news" media told me. At Tricky Dick's funeral, Henry Kissinger ended his eulogy by quoting... (Hell, sonny, you have a computer; you look it up)...somebody when he said, "We will never see his like again". Then Secretary Kissinger wept openly. Good enough for me.

GREEN NEW CONSTITUTION

Only the militia may keep and wear red hats if they bare the right arms of people at the

fringe of their 2nd commencement. If this makes sense to you, please buy soft towels and a loofah, shirts that button in the back, shoes that are too small, pads that are too big and, by all means, keep votin' Democrat.

I'M SORRY, SISTER ST. JOHN-OF-THE-HOLY-CROSS. I'LL BE GOOD!

The nuns wasted their time threatening us with the horrors of hell. All they hada do was say that there would be endless Adam Sandler movies.

How-will-YOU-spend-eternity?

GILLIBRAND GLOSSARY

Democrat: a dove when Trump deploys troops; a hawk when he withdraws them.

CNN: see "Democrat National Committee". It's the same thing.

Lib-ral democrat: puts the wants of every undocumented, unvetted, unvaccinated, unemployed, illiterate illegal alien invader, whose Country this ain't, over the safety and welfare of every hardworking, taxpaying* American citizen, whose Country this is. See also: "Archbishopric".

*Paying sales tax on cigarettes, tattoos, beer, and body piercings does not make you a "taxpayer". Tell Pocahontas.

SAVIN' YER ACHIN' BACK (AND YES, HOME ECONOMICS <u>IS</u> SEXIST)

If the garden hose blows out near the middle, you might want to get two couplings* rather than one union so you can make two 25 footers, which are damn handy when (if) you get old (older). If you need 50', why, they <u>do</u> screw together, Missy. **Note:** Yuppies should just throw the thing out and buy a new one, Gorewellian carbon footprint be damned. This is repair, Reba, not "reparations"; it'll only confuse ya.

*When choosing couplings, be sure to select one whose chosen (and <u>proven</u>) pronoun is "him", one "her". In the mechanical world, only males and females screw together. This annoys the crap outta the LGBT-WHATEVERS. Cool.

LOOKIN' FOR LOGIC

The first time I encountered a bra which hooked in the front I wondered why all didn't. Then I realized that they are worn by beings whose blouses button in the back. Hey Moe! We need more female engineers. Yea, that's it!

FIRST, THE AD SHOWED her driving while he minds the baby.

NOW, Mom comes home from work, finds Dad watching Oprah.

LEADERSHIP: THE BEST POLITICIANS MAKE THE BEST…POLITICIANS

He wanted to be different, and he was. Populist Jimmy Carter <u>walked</u> his inaugural parade. (Classy, long-suffering Roz wore low heels. Still, halfway through their tarmac trek, the Lady was <u>over it</u>.) Having no false hopes of draining the D.C. swamp, President-elect Carter decided to bypass it by bringing in his own people. This amused and annoyed the entrenched unelected career bureaucrats of both parties; they decreed that Carter wouldn't do shit. And he didn't.

Along comes Socialist Barack Obama, and Carter could have kissed him. When you start your stint with an apology tour, it follows that you ain't gonna do shit. And he didn't.

We all got kinder to Carter when he realized that Jimmy didn't do shit in 4 years, but Obama… I mean President* Obama, didn't do shit in 8. Overhaul our fucked-up foreign policy? Didn't do shit. Upgrade the lives of inner-city folks? Didn't do shit. Free North Korean hostages?** Didn't do shit. Improve race relations? Shit. President Obama sent "his wingman" (his words), United States Attorney General Holder and his henchmen to Fergusen lookin' for trouble. A dozen agents found no wrong-doing by the po-lice, and they sure tried to. President Obama could have calmed a Country by telling the truth: "hands up, don't shoot" <u>never happened</u>. But he didn't do shit. P.S: The only thing the black community should have said when thug/predator Michael Brown was taken out before he killed one of <u>them</u> was, "Thank you". But they didn't.

Enter Donald Trump. Building on the establishment-bucking mistakes of Nixon, Carter, and Reagan, Trump found a way to get shit done outside the purview of hostile Deep State operatives and their minions in the mainstream media. This drove never-Trump Republicans, Democrats, and the establishment "news" media out of their minds. (witness any broadcast on CNN, NBC, MSNBC, CBS, etc.)

Parody (learned this from Schiff): I can envision Trump's disloyal opposition putting the Country through a bogus 2-year collusion investigation which will be abandoned when it starts pointing toward Hillary. It would then not surprise me if desperate Democrats ditch democracy and drag the Nation through a year-long impeachment process rather than let We The People <u>vote</u> on the matter in, you guessed it, a year.

*No less a luminary than George Clooney, who pretends to be other people for a living, has schooled us that we may call Trump "Trump" but we must always and everywhere refer to Obama as "<u>President</u> Obama". (Yes, Pretender Clooney always says, "**President** Obama".)

**I still feel a twinge when I see the straw in the woodshed where my badass little bobcat used to sleep. Imagine how the Warmbiers feel every time they look into Otto's bedroom. Trump got the kid home, but too late. President Obama, you will recall, didn't do shit.

YOU CAN <u>RUN</u> WITH A WEEDEATER

They're up before dawn, and they notice <u>everything</u>. I'm thinking: "Farmers and hunters. Cool". Turns out, they're a-stir 'counta they're jonesing, alert 'cause they're looking for something to steal. Do-dah.

SMALL TOWN

You screwed up.

Q: How many days before the whole town's talkin' about it?

A: Five minutes.

MEDICATION CHIC MEETS COW DOG

Can't avoid meeting that pinch-faced yuppie down the block. She's gonna say, "This is a pure-bred Gran Dolor en el Culo; what is <u>that</u>?". I'll be able to announce, "**That** is a Doggus Bovinus bitch, and **she's** on Prozac".

On second thought, I'm gonna say, "**That** is a Doggus Bovinus, bitch..."

Tried one o' them Prozacs just to see what the attraction is, other than preventing Bones from chewing off her bandage. Bad stuff. Hada sit down to pee. Aarrgh...so <u>that's</u> why you gals want the seat down. Anyway, when it was time to get up, I couldn't. Woulda spent the night 'cept I feared I'd fall off and hit my head; didn't want <u>that</u> obit, so I slid off and made it to the dog bed. Real attractive. Luckily, Amazing Grace (or was it Dammit Janet?) had the dog that night.

EQUIPMENT

A gun is like a raincoat in that if you bring it and then don't need it, that is a Good Thing. If you need it but didn't bring it, now, don't YOU feel like an asshole.

Q: What's a perp say to a yuppie who brings a whistle to rape/robbery/etc.?
A: Now, don't YOU feel like an asshole.

NOT FOOD

I feared my body was getting low on its Monosodium Glutamate level, so I got a packet of Hidden Valley ranch dressing. Turns out, MSG is the fourth (4th) most prolific sclerotic in this chemical concoction. Hot Tip: chop some herbs to flavor sour cream, which by law cannot contain chemicals. Season to taste.

CRIMINALS

Packaging "engineers" should not be taken out and shot. Dog breeders should be taken out and shot. Packaging "engineers" should be taken out and hanged. On their own devices.

Plastic 6-pack rings have four (4) different size holes, the better to trap turtles with. (Not everybody cuts these things up.) Juice, jelly, rubbing alcohol, etc. are 2-packed via hard plastic rings courtesy of Pak Tech (PAKTECH-OPI.COM). These little horrors have <u>teeth</u> that add torture to slow strangulation of any small animal they ensnare. **Note:** The manufacturers who use these evil things have an 800 number for consumer comments. <u>Use it.</u>

Ladies only: You'll say, "Aw, poor thing", every time you see footage of yet another baby skunk, squirrel, raccoon, opossum, etc. with its head stuck in a container that looks as if it was designed to trap and suffocate small mammals, but you won't quit buying Yoplait yogurt because it comes in those small cutesy backwards cups that were designed just for you. We'd ask that you at least rinse them, but you put greasy pots in the dishwasher (with predictable results). "I am woman, hear me roar..."

ALBERTA GOREWELL

Commercial dishwashers run for one (1) minute 'cause Pepe' ain't afraid to rinse. Yuppie broad's machine takes an hour 'counta a quick rinse is beyond her. P.S.: Whining about <u>my</u> racegas "carbon footprint" isn't.

THEN HUG A TREE

Dumped a quart of milk? Reach for the Bounty. Saves r-r-rinsing out a rag (The horror!).

MUSLIMS AND OTHER MORONS

They tortured, raped, and killed her, but they wrapped her in a clean shroud.

With the dog gone, there was one less set of chores to do, so why did everything take longer? Fortunately for <u>you</u>, your little buddy was well-fed, well-walked, reasonably well-groomed, and **always** able to get out of the weather. That is your solace.

Losing any pet sucks, but for perspective, imagine what Otto's senseless death did to the Warmbiers, or how Kayla Mueller's defilement and murder affected her parents. Both were cut down while young by the stupidity of geopolitical maneuvering and, of course, Islam.*

*You tortured, raped, and murdered a young hospital worker. You think you are still tight with Allah because you gave her a "traditional Muslim funeral". Q: Is this lunacy or stupidty? A: This is Islam.

Note: The following "good Muslims" have condemned this atrocity:

Gillibrand Glossary:

Traditional Muslim Funeral: as they kick you into the hole, they simultaneously behead a heretic, drown a dissenter, and throw coupla queers off a building. Lighting and sound provided by someone who is being burned alive. Refreshments (non-alcoholic) will be served. Allah be praised.

MORE SOUTHERN FINE DINING: HOW TO EAT CHICKEN LIVERS

Shake off the breading. It is quite good. The end.

Q: What do you do with the liver? Feed it to the cat?

A: Only if you hate the cat.

Damnyankee chicken livers are gently sautéed in butter. Southern chicken livers are viciously deep fried in tractor awl. Used tractor awl. This makes a smooth organ go all pebbly. Imagine eating worms that have been fed aquarium gravel. Used aquarium gravel. Y'all.

~~NORTH FLORIDA~~ NORTHFLORIDA HOLLOW WEENIES

"We don't got nothin' for ya; we just like sittin' here seein' the costumes."

REPEAT THIS 100X EVER dang October 31. Wouldn't it be easier to get six bucks worth of Snickers? Y'all.

OK, THE CAT IS MY LITTLE BUDDY, but the dog was the glue that held it all together.

CELESTE AUTHENTIC ITALIAN PIZZA

Topping- imitation mozzarella (water, palm oil, potato starch). Swear to God.

##################GALA MURDER BY MUSLIM SECTION####################
FREEDOM OF CHOICE (**Gillibrand Glossary**)

Muslim: does not smoke, drink, or eat pork. Does throw queers off buildings, cut off infidel heads/drown them in cages/burn them alive. His choice.*

*Even Muslims' perverted freedom of choice does not include killing their own babies so late-term they are old enough to cry. Who are the monsters here?

Ps: Virginia's Governor <u>wants</u> to be able to deliver a baby and keep it "comfortable" while he chats with its Sanctity of Motherhood to see if she wants it killed. (Lib-rals will change the subject right...about...**here**.) If this is not infanticide, what is? **Note:** New York lib-rals actually applauded themselves when they passed a similar law. Monsters.

CNN RULES OF ENGAGEMENT (YA GOTTA HAVE RULES)
Skinheads burn a cross: news.
Muslims crucify a teen: not news.
Skinheads burn an Israeli flag: news.
Muslims burn an Israeli person: not news.
Chil-fil-a owner opposes gay "marriage": news.
Muslims throw queers off high buildings: not news.
No wonder CNN has to PAY the airports to carry this crap.

DOMESTIC TERRORISM

Gillibrand Glossary Woman: a being, some say sentient, who spies an 80 year-old rosewood-handled French chef's knife and thinks: "Yea, I'll just put this in the dishwasher".

Note: And why not? She's already run the cast iron skillet through it.

Q: Bro. Doesn't the skillet have 40 years worth of seasoning on it?
A: Not any more.

"BUT...BUT YOUR KITTEN (PUPPY, RABBIT, CHILD, ETC.) PROVOKED HIM!"

Congratulations to the breeders. They have developed a magical animal. All pit bull terriers morph into a "lab mix" the instant they tear off a child's face. They should all be taken out and shot.

Q: Ain't that a lotta dogs to shoot?
A: Talkin' bout the breeders.

A CROOKED LITTLE HOUSE

Woke wonkers have rendered our once-proud construction industry a bastion of imprecision. Try building something level, plumb, square and straight without telling your partner, "Just a cunt hair more".

IL PAPA FRANCISCO HYPOCRITO

"Let us build bridges, not walls." (The Vatican excepted, of course.)

AND I DIDN'T EVEN SAY, "THEY THROW QUEERS OFF BUILDINGS..."

You know you belong to a fucked-up religion when you feel compelled to kill anyone who worships differently, and your God thinks it's OK to torture and rape them first as long as you wrap their dead body in a clean white shroud. Att "liberals": I never said "Islam"; <u>you</u> did. Who is the Islamophobe here?

Gillibrand Glossary- traditional Muslim funeral: If you are a young hospital worker, you are shrouded and kicked into a unmarked hole in the ground so your parents will never find your corpse. If you are a beloved leader such as Ayatolla Khoumeni, you are carried through the streets of Teheran and allowed to slip from the bier and land in the street like a sack of shit. <u>Sign me up</u>. I want one of those.

YOU'RE GONNA DO <u>WHAT</u>

Hey, Moe! Let's market body bling that looks like snot hanging from your nose.

Q: Who'd buy <u>that</u>?

A: People with shirts that button in the back.

Q: How they gonna pay for something that SHOUTS "no money"?

A: They'll trade their food stamps, Silly.

Q: Won't We The Taxpayers be indirectly paying for her piercings?

A: Bro. We The Taxpayers already pay for her tattoos, beer, cigarettes, and five "free" phones for her five spawn via five dif'rent baby daddy. If this bothers you, you be a deplorable white racist sexist xenophobic pre-impeachment patriot who clings to his guns and his religion.

Gillibrand Glossary

Pre-impeachment patriotism: xenophobic, racist, and stupid.

Post-impeachment patriotism: impeachment.

Pre-impeachment Founders: racist old dead white men that we took out of schools.

Post-impeachment Founders: smart old dead white men who would want Trump impeached.

Source: every House Democrat

BACKLASH: THE PARTY OF THE WORKINGMAN...SAY <u>WHAT</u>?

"Nothing stops a bullet like a job". -United States Senator Kamala Harris

Kammy found out that her constituents would rather be shot at than w-w-work.

THEY MISSED THE "IRONY" CLASS. Charlie Kirk, <u>Campus Battlefield</u>
Her: Hon, Junior's college chums are coming over.
Him: Quick! Hide your red hunting cap, the Chic-fil-a cow, and my Rudyard Kipling collection.

YUPPIES ARE ALWAYS IN A HURRY
She puts a small pot on a large burner because she thinks it will heat faster. Meanwhile, she monitors my Mustang's carbon footprint. Cumbaya.

"NOTHING STOPS A BULLET LIKE A JOB." -Senator Kamala Harris (Did Kammy switch to Republican?)

\#
GALA YUPPIE SECTION
\#

Gillibrand Glossary

Yuppie: "This sucks. A young asshole has longer to <u>be</u> one."

Q: Is "Kirsten Phantomini" her real name?

A: Neither is "Gillibrand".

STORE BRAND

I thought ads shaming someone for paying a premium for her Prius were stupid until I inadvertently paid double for 6% sodium hypochloride, 94% water just because it said "Clorox" on the bottle. Rather than be thought an idiot (I have provided better reasons) I removed the label.

ZERO BRITA**

The live and work until they are 100 and die. The highlanders of Tibet eat clean meat and fresh vegetables; the water they draw from roiling, rock strewn mountain streams is so full of minerals* it looks like skim milk, which is another reason why we go to hunt camp off-season to repair the roof and escape the Bounty commercials. **Note:** Use a damp rag, stupid. For spilled drinks, rinse it (The horror!) and throw it in the washer. For greasy or nasty stuff, throw it out. Duh.

*Yes, the coffee it makes its...interesting.

**Brita is ancient Chaldean for "Yuppie".#

Yuppie is modern American for "Stupid".#

#Look it up.

WHAT WILL THEY LEARN WAITING TABLES?*

Even the wealthy should require their kids to work their way through school, at least part-time. Coddled college know-nothings are fodder for the leftist liberal hoaxes who pass for professors these days.

*To study well so they won't have to do this for a living.

WOMEN R TOUGH

Q: How do modern women, so concerned about greenhouse gasses, tolerate tub & tile mildew remover fumes?

A: Bro. Once you've had methyl-ethyl-keytone sprayed on your hair, and acrylic claws glued onto your fingernails, plain phosgene gas ain't no thing.

HOMOSEXUAL VS TWINKIE

Seeing the WTF look on my face, half of the burly "couple" cleared things up instantly and elegantly. "We're queer, not gay." 10-4.

A RACEBIKE EATS ASPHALT FOR LIVING, BUT A HORSE...

He paweth in the valley and rejoiceth in his strength: he goeth on to meet the armed men. He mocketh at fear, and is not affrighted; neither turneth he back from the sword. He swalloweth the ground with fierceness and rage. -Job 39:29-24

IT'S THE SAME CHICK: From biases and/or faces, can anyone tell Dana Bash and Andrea Mitchell apart?

GALA MATERNAL MISGIVING MISSIVE
################

WHY FRANKENSTEIN WAS TOUGH

The LGBT-WHATEVER "community" wants us to believe that a mutant male monster will one day birth a child. Hmmm. I wonder if it will be vicious enough to late-term abort its baby.

WHY SHIT HAPPENS

Pity the fool who doesn't believe in the Devil. He will never understand why, when things have a 50-50 chance of going wrong, they always do. Life's petty meannesses are less surprising when you acknowledge the omnipresence of Satan and realize that she <u>always</u> feels icky.

THE SANCTITY OF MOTHERHOOD

In Virginia, it is now legal for Mom to birth a baby and <u>then</u> decide to kill it. In New York, lib-ral legislators <u>applauded</u> themselves upon passing a similar bill so Doc and Mom can have a chat about What To Do with her latest mistake.

<hr>

"CHOICE" MEANS <u>ABORTION</u>, SILLY.

Conservatively-governed Florida's charter school students vastly outperform the attendees in public schools/child warehouses. Choice <u>works</u>, especially among poor and minority kids whose parents can now make informed decisions about their children's education. **How absurd.** Everybody knows that "choice" means offing your offspring up to the moment of birth and, in NY and VA, even later. "Choice" has nothing to do with educating a child that has survived a modern mom's maternal motivation to murder it. Ask any liberal.

P.S.: Charter schools are a clear and present danger to NEA (union, no competency testing) teacher-staffed schools' ability to indoctrinate America's youth into the wonderful world of dependence on gov-mint handouts.

...OR RISK NUCLEAR WAR FIVE DAYS A MONTH

Female candidates for President should be required to prove that they are post-menopausal. Vice Presidential candidates: no so much. We can risk a kicked-in copy machine or two, I mean, 48. (At the most: 96. -Editrix)

...AND A BURGLAR HAS FIVE LOCKS ON HIS DOOR.

Q: Why do convicted felons risk jail to carry a gun?
A: They know there are lotsa people out there just like them.
Q: Why do lib-rals bet their lives on a whistle?
A: Sheltered. (Street smarts Trump cumbaya-ism.)

HAIRCUT

Jesus was a badass. The Nazarene knock-off was not. When we tired of his ka-ra-TAY prattle, we tied him to the brass bar footrest. With his hair. Big-ass bouncer comes along to see WTF; we got real interested in our beer mugs. Never knew bars has scissors, but the guy came up lookin' like Jamie Lee Curtis.

ALL QUEERS SHOULD BE ISLAMOPHOBES. They're the ones who get thrown off buildings. (Straights just get beheaded.)

STEREOTYPE

The President of the United States throws brick after brick from the foul line.

Q: When does CNN cling to the canard that he is good at basketball?

A: When the president is black.

Q: Isn't that racist?

A: Bro. Only conservatives can be racists.

PS: The footage is now suppressed.

HON, WE'RE HAVING CHICKEN TONIGHT. BRING ME THAT SICKLY ONE.

Kentucky Pride was great. Even after it was bought out, things was good... until The Colonel died. Don't know which corporate conglomerate runs it now, but you know you're eating culled chicken when the drumstick bone is broken. Bon appétit. PS: the usta be best coleslaw is now just okay. Culled cabbage?

Contrast Chick-fil-A. Good from the start, it just gets better. Added advantage: while they're pullin' your order, you can get a gift card: perfect for your lib-ral professor. For a $5 card you get to watch this tenured Trotsky furtively scurry in to get his free sandwich. Greet him.

(This is not Maxine's cult of confrontation. A smile and a wave will do nicely.)

I CAN'T DRIVE 55: FLOORBOARDS & FRINGE vs FUCKING <u>FAST</u>

H-D riders are the brains of the motorcycling world. Riding a brakeless, ill-handling anachronism at 55 mph is damn scary; you don't <u>want</u> to go faster. A get-off at 55 ain't gonna kill you; hell, you'll probably walk away if you are wearing leathers, boots, gloves, <u>and a fucking helmet</u>.* I've never seen a headline says, "Man in gay pirate costume killed after crashing eight hundred pounds of Korean (assembled in USA, doncha know) scooter at near the poor thing's top speed.

At the Daytona Diner, the sultans of slow conspicuously park their contraptions** and make their entrance festooned with all manner of buckles, belts, buttons, bandannas, doodads, pins... needy crap that says, "Yeah. I ride."*** Meanwhile, the racers are quietly clad in sweatshirts and jeans.

* "I don't wear a helmet so I can hear danger coming." Bullshit. With straight pipes and a r-r-radio, you couldn't hear a train coming. You proffer your pate to the pavement so you can be <u>seen</u>, Tonto. Hot Tip: nobody gives a shit.

** That's it. Replace the vestigial suspension with "struts". For a <u>look</u>. There is no "form follows function" in this world. You will recall that Willie Davidson was kept on after the sellout as "Director of Styling". Gimme a break.

*** Stylin': "You know me by my habit."- Mountjoy

"Well, then, I know thee. What shall I know of thee?"-Henry V

Anyway, the Lord has a way of taking care of His 2-wheel idiots. One of the fastest guys I know is ungainly in the pits. I'll not mentioned Borge's name, but he just can't ride slow(ly). And if the posers on their pigs are having fun at a sleepy double-nickels, why take that away from them? I just wish they'd pay more attention to the ride and less to who's lookin' at them. If Mario Andretti made street racing a car seem stupid, well, Valentino Rossi put street motorcycle antics to death.

"Don't force your line. Take what the track gives you." - Borge Phantomini

"Why didn't you tell me that <u>before</u> I wadded up my bike? "-Phil Hurtso

SPARE THE ROD, RAISE A MONSTER: Your kid just caught a case because he never caught a spanking.

LIB-RALS CAN READ YOUR MIND

To a man (woman, undecided), the lib-ral focus group decreed ALL Trump supporters to be racist and stupid. This from people who think Kammy isn't black enough and that paintings of our country's "old, dead white men" (add ageism, necrophobia, and sexism) Founders should be removed from schools.

To me, racism <u>defines</u> a Party that views every aspect of our lives through a racial prism. Stupidity, of course, is hearing Maxine's ghettospeak or Nancy's gibberish and thinking: "Oh, yeah. <u>That's</u> what I look for in my elected representatives". Do-dah.

TRUMP IS AN IMMEDIATE DANGER. WE MUST IMPEACH <u>NOW</u>... The polls said <u>what</u>?

"For God. (Swear to God, they said that.) For the Founders. (You think I am making this up, don't you?) For our sacred honor. (Spoken with a straight face.) <u>For the children</u>." Huh? The polls are against... uh, nevermind. Bzzz. Za-appp.

NEIL GORSUCH SAID M-M-<u>MERRY CHRISTMAS</u>! THE HORROR!

Q: If "Merry Christmas" is a "Republican talking point", does "Happy Hanukkah" mean "kill A-rabs"?

A: Only at MSNBC.

ALOHA

Once away from the white-man-made slums of Oahu, the Hawaiian Islands are breathtakingly beautiful. Also charming are the many derivatives of the native language, which live on via many melodious words. "Lanai" is certainly nicer than the graceless English "porch", just as "wa-hi-ne" rolls off the tongue so much more elegantly than "teenage slut".

Editrix: What does Doctor Ford have to do with this?

ps: Doctor Ford is "afraid to fly", yet took many trips to Hawaii.

Q: Did Doctor Ford take the train to Hawaii?

A: Don't be ridiculous. Doctor Ford <u>pulled</u> a train in high school.

DICKLESS

Three midgets left the Guinness offices. "I won for the smallest hands!", guffawed the first. "I recorded the smallest feet!", gushed the second. "Who the hell is Adam Schiff?", groused the third.

PANDERING TO PARASITES (LIB-RALS GET THE LAST WORD)

Lib-ral: Legalize petty theft! The poor boost bread to feed their kids!

Sentiment being: Skag-heads steal stereos to feed their addiction.

Lib-ral: Addiction is a disease! Cumbaya!!!

Sentiment: All pricing includes loss due to theft. Translation: deadbeat depredations are on the backs of working people. Kinda like Congress.

Lib-ral: What are you, a c-c-conservative?

Also by Phil Berto

Snippets
Snippets: Comments from the Red
Snipped: America Post #Metoo
SNIPS: Comments from The Black and Blue
Snapped! Comments From a C-c-conservative

Watch for more at www.philberto.com.

About the Author

Phil Berto is a retiree with a wicked sense of humor and an old typewriter. When he isn't writing his thoughts to share with his fans and the rest of the world, he enjoys fishing, hunting and motorcycle racing, and finding new ways to annoy his lib-ral acquaintances.

Read more at www.philberto.com.

About the Publisher

Stormy Summers Publishing is a small publishing company that is dedicated to helping the Independent Author make it through those rough seas.